Stop Smoking EASY

The Definitive Handbook

How to quit smoking in a safe, lasting and easy way

HAN CARREL

ISBN 9798858503057

First Edition: 2017

© Copyright 2024 by Book Your Destiny - All rights reserved. The content contained within this book may not be reproduced, duplicated or transmitted without direct written permission from the author or the publisher. Under no circumstances will any blame or legal responsibility be held against the publisher, or author, for any damages, reparation, or monetary loss due to the information contained within this book; either directly or indirectly.

Cover: Frank Cant Layout: Yuki Yishida

All designs and pictures are property of Book Your Destiny or the source indicated

> **For any communication of curiosity, possible errors or inconvenience in using the book, you can send an email to support@bookyourdestiny.com one of our consultants will respond within 48 hours.**

Published by: www.bookyourdestiny.com

DISCLAIMER

Please note the information contained within this document is for educational and entertainment purposes only. All effort has been executed to present accurate, up-to-date, and reliable, complete information. No warranties of any kind are declared or implied. Readers acknowledge that the author is not engaging in the rendering of legal, financial, medical or professional advice.

WOULD YOU LIKE TO RECEIVE NEW BOOKS FOR FREE? Sign up now for our newsletter to receive new books and bonuses for free! (*Limited number of subscriptions*)

We are waiting for you!

TABLE OF CONTENTS

INTRODUCTION 8
COMMITMENT 11
USER GUIDE 12
1 HOW THINGS ARE 13
    The less pleasant news 15
    Addiction 15
    The power of addiction 17
    The smoker's inner discomfort 18
    Further consequences of smoking 19
    New opportunities 21
    It will not be easy 21
    What makes the difference 23
    The smoker and the smoking pattern 23
2 WHO I AM 25
    The beginnings 25
    Some testimony 26
3 THE PHASES OF THE JOURNEY 28
    Description of the phases 28
    What can happen 29
    You can do it 31
4 PREPARATION 33
    The idea of being a smoker 34
    Becoming free people 36
    The broken leg 37
    Reconditioning towards wellness 38
5 AWARENESS 39

A decision to make 40
Where are you 42
Tell me about you 43
Be a smoker or not 47
The 7 reasons why you keep going 50
Others quit on their own 52
A question of identity 54
The 3 identities 56
Willpower 57
The commitment 58
We are predisposed to the news 59
The smoker's resistances and the "dictatorship of habits" ... 60
Inner discomfort 62
The 3 beliefs 63
I smoke a few ones 67
If I want to, I'll stop by myself 68
Women, children and smoking 69
There is time 71
Training 71
Mass persuasion 72
Other aids 74
Lose weight without cigarettes 75
Abstinence 77
Trust or hope 80
How to notice the change 81
Accept the situation and yourself 84

6 MOTIVATION 88

The life I don't want 89

Something worthy living for 90

Thanks, but I don't smoke! 93

The Angel and the Demon 95

The intention to change 97

The past 98

The present 99

The future 99

Your motivation 100

Increase your motivation 101

Your goal 102

The great evil heals the little one 105

Your health gains 106

Economic management 110

Self-representation 110

Advantages of change 113

Enter K + ...115

A new environment of wellness 120

And if it were the last? 121

7 ACTION 124

Make your own rules 124

Do you smoke cigar or pipe? 127

The right moment 129

A question of balance 131

The cell and habit 131

Get out of your Comfort Zone 133

Go through the Discomfort Zone 135

5 key concepts to keep in mind 137

Improvement is change 139

Experience 139

There are no mistakes, there is learning! 140

Cigarette and body weight 141

Time travel 143

"Electronic cigarette" and nicotine substitutes 148

The business of smoking 149

The cigarette substitutes 151

Focus 152

David's story 153

Now it's up to you! 154

The structure of wellness 156

The three main areas 157

When do we get free? 160

Talk to your stimulus 162

A new way of life 163

Get involved in some activity or hobby 166

Change habits to feel good 167

Mental reconditioning 168

A small commitment 169

Muscle Response Test 171

8 RECONDITIONING 174

Things to do 175

Stratagems 176

Techniques 178

Time distortion exercise 178

Get used to making decisions 181
The "timeless" 182
Accept difficulties 185
The emotions 186
Only one 195
First you and then me 196
Observe and interview 198
Become a master 199
DOWNLOAD YOUR FREE BONUS 201
CONCLUSION 202
AUTHOR 205

DISCLAIMER

The details in this book have informative, dissemination and guidance purposes and do not constitute medical advice in any way.

In case of doubt, you should consult your doctor.

All the links, free resources and suggestions indicated in the appropriate section have been included because considered potentially useful for the reader. However, further personal research is suggested to deepen the themes and topics of greatest interest. The author has no responsibility for the use of related information.

ACKNOWLEDGMENTS

Heartfelt thanks to the hundreds of thousands of people who have entrusted themselves to this book.

INTRODUCTION

We were on our third meeting and John kept talking about his parents, his family, his friends and his problems, or rather, everything that was bothering him but not about the reason why he was staying with me: the smoking. Although he was aware of hurting himself, he could not stop. This put me in crisis, I thought I was not able to help him, not to make it. John was one of my first clients and in the next ten years, despite the inevitable difficulties, I would have learned that by providing the most appropriate support and strategies, along with the commitment of the person, anyone can quit and permanently free themselves from smoking.

The fight against smoking has led to a knowledge of the phenomenon that today provides the best possible preparation: studies, experiments and concrete results on millions of people. We know how our brain and body work, how our mind-body system gets sick and, above all, how it can improve, get healthy and stay there. We have at our disposal supports such as drugs, techniques and psychological strategies that were unthinkable until a few years ago.

What is the cigarette used for? What is the role it plays in a smoker's life? Why do you smoke? Have you ever asked yourself certain questions? From my own experience with smokers, I have been able to understand that part of the solution lies in answering these questions.

When you understand *why*, you will be at a good point.

Another part of the challenge concerns *what* to do to permanently get rid of from smoking. And another one is *how*, which consists of the whole strategies and techniques to be applied, in order to transform concrete action into new wellness habits. In turn - this is the crux of the matter - creating new habits leads to an improvement in the level of personal well-being. By habit I mean a pattern rooted within us, which starting from a stimulus - sensations and thoughts - translates into a certain behaviour.

What I was wrong with John was just that: we acted on behaviours without dwelling enough on how they are generated and how they can be changed. We only worked on some conscious aspects and not on the submerged world that is inside each of us.

John, like every smoker I have known and know, was not stupid, on the contrary, he was a very smart person; therefore, the solution was not at the cognitive level (of reasoning), but much more deeply. I have developed this text with this assumption by putting together all the techniques and strategies I have used with my clients.

Some recommended steps are required for the book's content to be truly effective. The first is to call things by their name, in order to tell you what's going on, without turning around to be delicate or avoid offending some particularly sensitive or touchy smoker: smoking, or it would be better to call it tobacco addiction, is an addiction, a pathology.

Specifically, it belongs to the category of "substance use disorders". This is not my personal judgment: doctors and scholars express themselves in these terms[1]. So I warn you that you may not like my sometimes direct and crude ways and expressions. However, besides being my acquired style, this way of speaking is very powerful and effective for you in this context. I know from experience that the smoker prefers a direct, decisive, sometimes harsh language, because being it is a book, he does not take it personally - which instead happens in the face-to-face comparison - and he recognizes and accepts even some "uncomfortable" truths willingly.

Secondly, you must follow some necessary steps to get rid of smoking, the 4 phases of the path that I illustrate in this book and that will lead you to freedom.

In the first stage, awareness, we will know the smoking and addiction's background. You will be able to observe your connection with the cigarette from a new and different point of view. We will build new perspectives and offer useful information.

In the second phase, motivation, we will highlight what you will lose and gain by freeing yourself from cigarettes, what you can do and why.

The third phase, action, focuses on what to do, how to do it and on the practical application of strategies in order to dismantle the psychological traps that keep you anchored to the cigarette.

In the last phase, reconditioning, I will ask you to implement exercises and gradually integrate new habits into your daily life that could replace the cigarette

---

[1] The disorder is considered mild based on the persistence of several symptoms over a period of 12 months. For further information, cf. F. Cosci, V. Zagà, "Tobacco in the DSM-5", «Tabaccologia», 2014, 1-2, p. 7; http://www.tabaccologia.it/filedi-rectory/Tabaccologia_1-2_2014.pdf

and contribute to your physical and mental wellness. When I talk about *reconditioning*, I mean that you will change your way of life compared to the setting you have maintained so far: the habit of smoking and everything that concerns it will be unhinged to make space for a new life style focused on well-being. Yourself will identify what is most suitable for you, you will be the real authors of your improvement, choosing it and working hard to make it concrete in your daily actions.

Maybe you will get the impression that I tend to repeat myself or that some exercises are similar. But whether it is your consideration or reality, everything is organized to allow you to obtain the best result.

The repetitions are used to reinforce the steps that may be more challenging.

The path that I propose here is free from health risks. However, I must point out that smoking causes changes in our body and, in the first period, you will feel the lack of cigarettes even physically. So, if you experience symptoms that do not convince you, describe the situation to your doctor, pointing out that you are following a path for tobacco deconditioning. If you follow the path with commitment, I guarantee you that you will win the challenge and gain in wellness for you and your loved ones.

Each of you can do it, in a safe, simple and lasting way.

Good trip!

Carrel Han

P.S. You can read this book and put the tips into practice even if you are following other tobacco deconditioning treatments. Although the path that I propose here is focused on personal growth, it can be enhanced by integration with already elaborated methodologies.

COMMITMENT

1. Don't passively believe what I say and write in this book. What I write is *not* the law, not everything is valid for you. I don't have the magic sphere; I can only suggest a pattern that has proven effective on many people. Thousands of smokers have achieved the desired results, but you must put in the effort and test yourself, try it for yourself.

   Don't passively believe what I say and write in this book.

   Prove yourself too!

2. Commit to follow our work together, give your 100%. The result you get depends on how much you work hard: from doing, not doing, doing mediocrely. In order to get the best result apply this rule to every page of this book: be 100% committed!

   Commit to this work together, word hard!

3. Read with a child's curiosity. With his innocence and carefreeness. Remember when you used to play with other children? You were free, without prejudices or patterns, you just did things, just for pleasure.

Blank pages on which you can write new points of view. So read freely, without pre-established patterns.

Be curious and free like a child!

I ....**Karen**.................... I accept and confirm the conditions described above (1., 2., 3.)

Date ...**29/4/23**...   Sign ....*(signature)*....

USER GUIDE

This book has been studied in detail to help you reach your purpose, which is why it is sometimes repetitive like a smoker: it convinces, persuades and educates to wellness. It appeals and stimulates the best part of you. So, read it very calmly, spreading the reading over several days, so that you can reflect and metabolize the concepts and, at the same time, avoid stress. Take a moment of your own to answer the questionnaires you will find. If you are using the paper version, use the spaces provided to answer the questions. You can also write the answers on a separate sheet in the first instance, but before completing the reference chapter, be careful to write them down right in the book. Why do I insist so much? Because re-reading your answers will allow you to follow the evolution of the journey you have taken, making our work together much more effective. Write in pencil so that you can review and improve the content later. Avoid skipping the exercises with the excuse that they appear similar but repeat the ones you think are most useful for you. Respect your inner times and go back to the pages that inspired you the most in order to clarify, assimilate and reinforce the concept. Without sacrifice, but with the awareness of wanting to find one's balance without a cigarette. Finally, a brief explanation of the abbreviations that you will encounter in correspondence with some of the exercises.

Figure 1 Press and hold index finger and thumb of the right hand

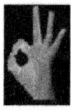

Figure 2 Press and hold index finger and thumb of the left hand

Figure 3 Muscular Answer Test Position to maintain

1 HOW THINGS ARE

The smoke cages

Let's be honest: I could start by listing all the harm caused by the smoking, but what good would it be? I want to offer you a new point of view, a new broader and clearer perspective on the problem, providing you with data, observations from the former smokers and direct experiences that stimulate reflections focused on well-being in you. I'm not here to lecture you or repeat speeches that you may have heard hundreds of times. My intention is another: I want to create a dialogue that brings you new elements, pushing you to consider the issue of smoking, and your life, from another perspective. And then, honestly, did the so infamous lectures ever take effect? Looking around, I would say no.

How often do you see smokers with parents who are also smokers? Often. In fact, statistically it is easier for children of smokers to become smokers themselves. This phenomenon is based on the principle of imitation. This may not have been the case for you, however in most cases I can assure you that it is. Many times I have happened to hear from a parent or a grandfather: "Now I can't stop anymore, but he mustn't smoke." You understand well the inadequacy of such a will. The state itself bans smoking in some places, promotes anti-smoking campaigns and then sells cigarettes. Just as it allows "gambling" and, at the end of the advertisement, with the speed typical of warnings on medicines, it inserts the message: "Gambling is forbidden to minors, it can cause pathological addiction". Do you think it does this for the health and wellness of its citizens? Of course not, otherwise it would not sell certain "services" and "products": it is only a matter of legal protection against any claims for damages. In the book *Helping to quit smoking? It's easier than you think*[2], Fabio Lugoboni writes:

> «In Italy the percentage of doctors who smoke is variable: in a study conducted a few years ago on 983 specialists in pulmonology, 26.5% were smokers. Male doctors smoke as much as other graduates [...]

---

[2] F. Lugoboni, *Helping to quit smoking? It's easier than you think*, Edizioni Seed, 2012, Turin, p.17.

while female medical graduates smoke more than graduates in other disciplines, accounting for 42% in a study of medical graduates in Southern Italy. [...] The United States, which has made the fight against smoking a priority health goal, is a country where only 2% of doctors smoke (same prevalence as the United Kingdom) and where a patient will never see their doctor if it belongs to that narrow minority of smokers, to light a cigarette».

In such a context it becomes difficult to distinguish good from bad, right from wrong, well-being from malaise. We are hit by a myriad of misleading messages every day: from advertisements, ù bad and manipulative information, and often also from family upbringing with learned habits, to the point that what others do seems normal to us, even if it regards incorrect behaviours that damage ourselves and the community. Today we must expect clarity where others prefer not to give us: the more confused and manipulated we are, the better they can control us and the more they can earn. On the other hand, we can decide to choose in an intelligent and conscious way and not be "influenced" by induced needs: in addition to being a little exercised right, it is a power we have over our life. Smoking is a symptom, a manifestation of malaise, a kind of alarm. Otherwise, at the same time, it aggravates the already labile mental situation. Then, you add the daily stress, and the problem grows like a snowball that becomes an avalanche downstream.

What do you want to communicate with smoking?

Smokers have a false sense of control and tension release. It is overloading a system that could collapse at any moment. Day after day, the habit of smoking is consolidated and leads to addiction, which over time breaks the barriers, invading every aspect of a person's life. Thus was born the smoker, who in addition, by creating and strengthening an addictive personality, tends to generalize the subjection towards life. Smoking, therefore, comes from a situation of malaise and continues to feed and strengthen it. For some, smoking is a self-punishment mechanism, for others self-destruction, for others a request for attention. Then, there are those who say they love each other and smoke. Of course this is not the case. Do you also know people who say they love each other but adopt behaviours opposite to the wellness of the mind and body? Among them I have met many smokers and all of them lie, not only to others but, above all, to themselves. Those who smoke do not love themselves.

The less pleasant news

Behind the cigarette there are insecurity, anger, fear, frustration. The smoker goes to great lengths in order to prove otherwise. Behind the cigarette lies the sense of helplessness, the fear of not being considered important, of not being seen. The cigarette is a mean that allows the child inside the adult to be noticed, to be taken into consideration, to feel great when they are not yet. Imagine having a cigarette in front of you. How big is the cigarette compared to your person? Many smokers see a giant cigarette in front of them. Try it, imagine a huge cigarette in front of your eyes: it is likely that you too feel an unpleasant and almost helpless feeling too. Internal representations tell us a lot about how we perceive reality, how we experience it and who we are. But it is not the cigarette that becomes giant, it is the smoker who feels small. This status could occur in everyday life.

To the question: «What does smoking mean for you, what do you need it for, what result do you think you will achieve in relation to others? », a client, after some time of reflection, replied: «I feel terrible, I want to hurt myself and I want that the others know! Maybe I want more attention and consideration! ».

Since this episode, I have adopted a very powerful strategy that you can follow too. From today, whenever you have a cigarette between your fingers, repeat in your mind: «I feel terrible, I want to hurt myself and I want others to know! I want more attention and consideration! ».

I know that this "mantra" does not reflect the characteristics of all of you, it is just an example. You can create your own very well and replace it. But if it is not easy for you, start with this: it has worked for many. Some, after repeating this sentence with every cigarette, began to no longer feel that pleasure, and somehow recognized that some aspects really concerned them. So they personalize to this mantra with personal adjustments. Smoking establishes a mechanism that generates further stress and nervousness, with the consequence of being tempted to smoke even more cigarettes in an even more intense way. So, our personal energies are strongly affected by this principle of change: we tire and stress excessively, and the simplest things get complicated.

Addiction

So let's begin to delve into the question and clarify the many wrong information that exists about addiction, starting from the very meaning of the term. In order to do this, I report here (and in other parts of the book) parts from an interesting article written by Johann Hari, author of *Chasing the Scream: The First and Last Days of the War on Drugs*[3]:

> «If you had asked me some time ago what the origin of drug addiction was, I would have looked at you like idiots, and I would have said: "Well, drugs, right?". It wasn't difficult to understand. I was convinced that I had experienced it first-hand. We are all able to explain it. Suppose you and I, along with the next twenty passers-by, are determined to administer a truly potent drug for twenty days straight. Because these drugs have strong chemical hooks, if we stop on the twenty-first day, our bodies will end up craving that substance. A fierce greed. We would then become addicted to it. This is what 'addiction' means. The theory was partly codified thanks to experiments carried out on mice - which entered the American collective psyche in the 1980s thanks to a well-known advertising campaign by Partnership for a Drug-Free America. You may remember it. The experiment is quite simple. Put a mouse in a cage, alone, with two bottles of water. One contains only water. The other also heroin or cocaine. Almost every single time the experiment is repeated, the mouse will end up obsessed with the drugged water and will come back to ask for more until the moment he dies. The ad put it this way: "There is only one drug that can induce so much addiction, and nine out of ten laboratory mice will use it. Yet. It's still. Till death. It is called cocaine. And he can do the same to you"».

There is nothing scandalous in being dependent on something or someone, we all are, some more, some less and in different forms. It is a fact related to our survival. Be careful, I'm not saying that drug addiction is good, as well as cigarettes are. I am telling you instead not to look at the behaviour, but to dwell on the pattern behind it.

When a baby comes into the world, he is totally dependent on his mother: without her, he would die. So addiction is a fact of life, and it exists as a relationship. We are all dependent on someone or something, and the existence of someone or something depends on us. If reciprocal, it is better defined as

---

[3] Hari, "La più probabile causa della dipendenza è stata scoperta – e non è ciò che credete", «Huffington Post», 24/01/2015, http://www.huffingtonpost.it/johann-hari/la-piu-probabile-causa-dipendenza_b_6537964.html

interdependence. So, what's the difference with smoking, drugs, if all of us are addicted to someone or something in some way?

First point: awareness. It is important to know what or on whom we depend, and to make sure that there is reciprocity, in a system of interdependence. Otherwise, someone who is addicted to someone or something simply demonstrates that they have a very low opinion of themselves! Second point: it is desirable that what one depends on is nourishment, as was breast milk. A relationship is healthy only if it allows you to grow and improve, if it leaves room for independence. If you think about it, none of the drugs - cocaine, nicotine, heroin, alcohol, etc. - pushes towards addiction, indeed: these substances raise the bar of the dosage, they ask for increasingly more. There is no reciprocity.

The power of addiction

During some personal growth events, I like to tell the story of a baby elephant - a kind of giant stuffed animal that generates a feeling of tenderness just thinking about it - who is trained to become a circus attraction. At first, listening to his verse makes you smile. By looking closer, you notice a large chain tied on one side to a leg and on the other end to a large pole. The puppy is trapped, forced to stay within a range of action that someone has decided for him.

Who knows what sensation the baby elephant feels inside himself...!

How would you feel?

As he grows up, bound by the large chain that keeps him tied to the pole, he is convinced that his whole life must take place within that circle. Over time, trainers replace the large chain with a thin rope. The elephant is an adult now, it could break the rope simply with a small movement and without any effort. However, he does not, because he is convinced that it is impossible. His life, his world, are within that circle, because he knows nothing else, except that circle. For above to live, he just must accept and defend the situation, rejecting whatever is different. All that is outside does not fit into his world and therefore he rejects it. He begins to say to himself: "It is because world works like this", "There is nothing I can do to change the situation", "In life you have to be satisfied", "There is worse", "I am like this and I cannot change", etc. Every day the elephant repeats these things to himself. Every single day.

And what do you repeat in your head every day? "I can't stop!", "I like it!", "It gets worse!", "It's impossible now!" ... Actually, smokers do not know freedom. All the smokers I met were prisoners of a mental pattern (not only them, of course):

they did not know how to choose their own life independently. there was always the voice of "someone" inside them who said what to do and how to behave, including prohibitions, restrictions, impositions, feelings of guilt and anger. If you want to get out of a pattern that you recognize as limiting, the only way is to find the courage to be free, choose, act without any constraint. When we say we are free to decide, we sometimes make fun of ourselves. There are those who have never chosen until today, but now would like to take their lives in hand. Start doing what makes you feel good: live the present moment to the fullest, facing the future wellness. Smoking, bad relationships and negative people are not part of this game. Cultivate healthy and positive relationships, commit yourself. Learn to do it.

Write below the excuses (and/or false beliefs) that justify the fact that you smoke. Think of the ones you repeat most often: "I smoke because I like it", "I smoke because I'm too stressed", "I smoke otherwise I get fat", "I smoke because it helps me to concentrate", "I smoke to have an escape valve", "I smoke because it is the only vice I have", etc. Take the pen and write:

I smoke because I enjoy it.

I smoke because I feel it relaxe's me.

I smoke because it is a habit

I smoke because I think I will become depressed if I don't.

Big energy = Big opinion of yourself = Freedom

Create the most useful inner environment for change.

The smoker's inner discomfort

I remember a friend of mine years ago. We went into a nightclub, and after three minutes we were inside, he said to me: "Let's go to the bar and drink something." His way of expressing himself was not accidental, he really needed something between himself and others. He did not smoke, otherwise he would have come in with a cigarette in hands. He would have turned it on between the car and the nightclub's entrance, as I have seen friends and strangers do so many other times. The smoker feels a particular difficulty in relating to others, he feels a discomfort. Johann Hari, referring to Professor Peter Cohen, explains that human beings have a deep need to form bonds and encounter each other. We all need the sense of gratification that derives from relationships. And if we are unable to get in touch with others, we will meet anything else: the sound of a spinning wheel, or the needle of a syringe. Hari believes that we should stop talking about "addictions", and rather call them "ties". A heroin addict bonds with heroin because he has not been able to tie strongly with anything else; so does the smoker with the cigarette.

Therefore, on one hand, the drive to relate is inherent in each of us; on the other hand, relationships make us vulnerable. In fact, our internal tension increases before and during contact with others; it can be applied to everyone, regardless of smoking. In public places, at meetings, on occasions when people meet, the fear that they may judge and reject us can arise. Then, the cigarette acts as a mediator. It is a useful prosthesis for many smokers in order to take time between one speech and another, filling in empty moments, reflecting on what to say and how to break the ice in new encounters, in situations where you want to take new directions and break the tension. It happens to everyone to feel uncomfortable in the downtimes of a conversation, especially with people who do not know each other. It happens to me too, but I try to see things from another point of view: in those moments, there are two or more, which means that perhaps the other party is also afraid of being judged and feels the same sensations just like us. It is a mutual fact. Thinking about it, there is no reason, but it happens, it is an unconscious mechanism; perhaps not with everyone, but with some people and in certain situations, the fear of the others' judgment comes back. Yet, think about it, do you constantly judge your interlocutor if there is any downtime in the speech? Most certainly not. So, why should this happen to you? Why lean on the cigarette excuse?

Further consequences of smoking

At this point, you will have understood that the cigarette is a symptom, it is the result of a routine of thoughts, emotions and actions. The real cause of smoking addiction lies in having a low energy and consideration of oneself. You lack control over your life, folding over your cigarette. Smoking is a ritual: it has the function of marking the day. The ritual is a compass, which tells us that we are a little ahead of yesterday. Think of birthdays, holidays, dinners, lunches, times set by society: they are all rituals. If you follow them, everything is going well, otherwise not. This is how we work. Rituals create meaning, just as the cigarette creates the illusion of moving forward. Allen Carr, popular all over the world for the book *È facile smettere di fumare se sai come farlo4*, not surprisingly uses the image of the tapis roulant. Smoking gives the sensation of moving forward while remaining stationary. It's like packing your suitcases for a trip, while staying closed at home. The journey remains in the head, while one stays still a prisoner.

I do not want to launch futile alarms or blame anyone, but I also invite you to evaluate aspects that you may not have known up to now, in order to seriously consider the repercussions of smoking on your life and on those who surround you. Cigarettes can also be the gateway to "joint", alcohol, and even cocaine, heroin and other tragic addictions. Not that smoking itself is not dangerous, be careful, but the statistics support what I say. Those who take drugs, drink alcohol and smoke. Have you ever seen an alcoholic who does not smoke? A junkie who does not smoke? According to a research conducted by the ASL of Milan 3 in 2006, as many as 95% of drug addicts smoke5. You must consider also the typical social environment: smokers tend to have a low opinion of themselves, to be together, to create a group of peers, a vicious circle. I am concerned about young people. Adolescents activate a request for help through the cigarette. They want to communicate something to adults. It means: "I live badly, I have a discomfort". Parents should be aware of their children's malaise: smoking is one of the most obvious symptoms. The example starts with adults, parents and socially influential figures. If you are executives, doctors, state officials, actors or actresses, people respected and followed by thousands of people, leaders, you should not smoke. Adults are responsible for young people. Learning is based on direct experience, but, above all, on the imprinting provided by the context and the modelling regarding the way of being and behaving. According to recent neurological studies, learning takes place by imitation: the era of "Do what I say and not what I do" is over.

In addition to the problem of social models, think of the damage to the quality of life and the environment. The environment suffers incalculable damage every day due to cigarette stubs thrown on the street, on the beach, in the woods. It is not a simple matter of decorum; it is about protecting our well-being by safeguarding the environment in which we live. The "stubs" pollute like industrial waste. City manholes get clogged. Beaches are the largest ashtrays on the planet. Entire forests disappear to make space for immense tobacco crops,

---

4 A. Carr, Allen Carr's Easy Way to Stop Smoking, 1985.

5 B. Tinghino et al. , "Tabagismo: dipendenza "minore"? Correlazioni tra dipendenza da tabacco e uso di sostanze stupefacenti", «Tabaccologia» 2006, 1, pp. 23-25, http://www.tabaccologia.it/PDF/1_2006/7_1_2006.pdf

others due to negligent fires caused by a simple cigarette. Not to mention the health and social costs of addiction, and all the phenomena of impoverishment, exploitation of workers, crime and smuggling combined to the production and sale of tobacco. These are all aspects that we cannot afford to ignore.

New opportunities

Today we all have a great need for change, serenity and concrete results. We are tired and we want more in terms of wellness all-around. Nonetheless, we often tend to replicate unhealthy and unproductive habits. But, if you are leafing through this book, it means that you would like to change something in your life too. Quitting smoking is a good start. If you want to have the best, you will have to roll up your sleeves and strive to achieve those results that are important to you, for you and those around you. I will put at your disposal the best knowledge I could acquire in this field in order to help you. You give us the right motivation. Demand the best. You will certainly have a strong desire to change, you will be tired of the constraints imposed by old patterns which, on the one hand, give a (false) security but, on the other hand, trap us. The cigarette is one of this mechanism's manifestations, perhaps the most evident and measurable. In fact, let us remember that the bond with the cigarette is not only physical, but it also has to do with a change of mentality. If you desire improvement within yourself, although it is still difficult for you, start thinking in these terms. Get used to the idea and look for an upgrading in everything you do. Avoid dwelling on what you do not have, what you have not obtained or what you think we have taken off even though you are entitled to it. It is useless, because the past is over. You will often hear this expression in the book. Just dwell on what you have, how to fully enjoy it and how to add value to your life. I repeat you are not here simply to throw a cigarette; you are here to become a better person!

It will not be easy

It will not be easy, although I will suggest step by step what needs to be done. You will begin to suffer from abstinence, feeling unwell, it is normal. You will miss the cigarette, especially at times when you used to abuse it. You will be tempted by other smokers. You will feel discomfort in situations that you previously faced with a cigarette between your fingers, it will seem impossible to manage them without. You will automatically put your hands in your pockets to look for one, even without having bought them. Maybe you will not sleep at night. Everyone reacts in a different way. However, I assure you that, if you follow the steps I suggest, you will succeed. Maybe for someone, it may take a few more weeks or months, for others just a few days. It does not matter: the essential thing is to believe in it, moving forward despite everything.

The difficulties that are generally encountered are not real, or rather, they are based more on self-limiting beliefs: "I can't do it", "This is not the right time", etc. Sometimes it is hard to come face to face with one's weaknesses; for this reason, I will suggest specific exercises that will help you overcome the discomfort and will be able to make you feel stronger. The path that you have already started in part is very simple; however, I have made it more complex to ensure that your commitment is more attentive and focused. By complicating things for you right away, I make them much simpler and effective in the long run, so that you can truly be free.

Warnings

If you think to read this book as if it were a novel, without focusing on doing the exercises, or without rereading and revising some chapters, then yes it will be hard. The habits you are naturally attached to will want to stay alive, they will not so easily leave space for new and more productive behaviours. And, although you may suffer from the abandonment syndrome, with your habits a part of you will also change, which will no longer be there, being replaced by a better one. In some passages it will take more time and effort for you to succeed in the new reflection, in the change of perspective. So, do not be discouraged, continue, because you will initiate a process that will emerge during the rest of the book in any case, or in the re-reading of some parts. Many things in your life will change, for example relationships with friends: you will feel the desire to renew your knowledge, maybe eliminate some or change some dynamics of the existing ones. The challenge will be to let go and "lose" what you are used to, and which somehow gives you the confidence to gain much more value for yourself and your family.

I would like to explain to you more clearly how I wrote this book. It is evident that I generalize throughout the writing of the words. This is for the convenience of exposure and, above all, because as I write I have in mind the Smoker, a figure that encompasses the discomforts, needs, uncertainties, patterns and beliefs of the thousands of smokers I have personally met. Therefore, you can use the same techniques and tools of thousands of smokers who are non-smokers today and that I have put together over the years. All these techniques have in common a "success strategy", which acts on three closely related areas:

1. mental

2. emotional

3. behavioural.

What makes the difference

What makes the difference is the type of approach. Most people try to remedy the difficulties, focus on the wrong behaviour, try to correct it but with little - or even no - lasting results, as is often the case with diets. Instead, our goal is to dig deeper and replenish that ability to develop well-being received at birth. The difference between a smoker and a non-smoker in fact lies precisely in the structure of one's wellness, in the way in which the thoughts, emotions and behaviours that revolve around this focal point are organized over time. Those who want to "quit smoking" and get rid of cigarettes do not have to think about how to "cure" a disease or solve a problem; he must focus only on the structure of his own well-being. For this reason, the expression "quit smoking" is inappropriate, because it focuses on the problem and not on the solution, which consists in establishing new and healthy wellness habits. However, I often use "quit smoking" for convenience and common language.

The smoker and the smoking pattern

Most people learn their model of family well-being from his childhood onwards. Some learn healthy patterns, others harmful, sometimes even destructive. Either way, we learn how to live from our models.

> *Smoking is a behaviour that starts from thoughts: it is an inadequate response to external solicitations, driven by sensations.*

The most interesting thing for me – and I assure you above all for the smokers I followed – was that of not being able to understand how it was possible not to feel any desire anymore. How can we not recognize an advantage when it is evident? It cannot be done!

Based on my experience, I am almost certain that many are unable to perceive the benefits of quitting smoking.

Let's be clear: it is not a real inability; it is rather a question of focus and attitude. I can assure you that protecting your well-being will increase your self-esteem: achieving a great result is always a great victory.

2 WHO I AM

I approached the problem of smoking addiction because as a coach and trainer I have always been interested in the topic of habits and changes. Smoking was a challenging and successfully overcome fight from which I realized that smoking is not foolish, if anything it is to start. Smoking is serious, a real addiction.

The beginnings

About fifteen years ago, I worked as a trainer for a company operating in the sales sector, dealing with staff training, employee management and skills development. In short, I followed the collaborators in their personal and professional improvement, a key aspect for the business' growth. What does this talk have to do with helping people to quit smoking? It has to do with the extent to which my task was pushing people to improve, change, achieve goals. Doing my job better, I had to persuade and motivate customers and collaborators. And I succeeded with good satisfaction. So well that at times I triggered, in a not completely conscious way, or rather, not having decided a priori, a profound change in their behaviour, in their life. I realized that I was able to "manipulate" some situations obtaining a change of the person in a very short time. A collaborator with whom I was in close contact at the time revealed to me, after a few months that he no longer smoked, that it was me, who "triggered the click" and pushed him to stop smoking during a meeting. After accidentally helping my colleague to quit, I continued with many other people. I realized that "smoking" was not a subject to be taken lightly. I had underestimated, or perhaps never seriously considered, the tragedy of this addiction. I thought smokers were just stupid up until that point. It was not like this. I found myself faced with the greatest addiction of our day and perhaps ever. I remember that one day I went into a bar to have a coffee and I began to discuss the subject of cigarettes, which was starting to interest me with the people present. Speaking of the smoking's damage, I pointed out that cigarettes are also a cause of impotence in humans. A lady known to say the least "gallant" in that circumstance felt compelled to protect the category, saying that her sexual experience with smokers had always been exceptional. I do not tell you how small I felt, I wanted to disappear. But it was useful to me to understand that the smoker has the need - I would say physiological - to defend smoking even more than the need to smoke itself. In order to date, I have never encountered such resistance that it can be compared to the smokers' one. Any other person addicted to substance use usually has a perception of personal and social problems such as to admit to being a prisoner of them, not being able to do without them and declare to be addicted to.

The smoker, on the other hand, does not give up because he does not perceive the cigarette problem with the same gravity.

A new human and professional challenge

Until then, I had never thought about using what I did, and knew, to help people quit smoking. But basically it was still about helping others improve. So, I started as a "game" to convince smoking friends to get rid of smoking... and it worked! "If it works and then they are fine thanks to you," I said to myself "do it!" So, I started studying the subject and deepening the subject of communication and coaching strategies relating to smoking. Every day I practiced the smoker's persuasion with whoever I met. "Because-I-like" have always been my favourite. The "I-will-never-stop" too. I applied my strategies for free and refined them over time. I studied and applied. I stimulated and persuaded to quit. 68% of the people who came to meet me were able to free themselves from the cigarette in a short time. Some in an hour, after just one appointment (they certainly put my suggestions into practice even later). Others after a few weeks, still others spent a few months. Within a year of quitting, only 35% of them had resumed smoking, making new meetings necessary. However, of the latter only 50% had started smoking again as before, the other part "smoked" - I quote the expression of one of them - only a few cigarettes a day.

Some testimony

Great are the satisfactions and successes I have met in helping others to quit smoking. The greatest gift was seeing their eyes and smiles full of light, of different people, more self-confident, satisfied, who have regained great energy.

I want to give you some testimonials, among the hundreds that I have collected over time. I am very attached to the first one, Frank's one: a nice person, dedicated to the family and eager to get better. The testimony dates to 2006, but the meetings had taken place two years earlier. A genuine and spontaneous one.

Unfortunately, I recently learned that Frank has passed for a few years, and so I wanted to remember him in this book.

Name: Frank Age: 63 Profession: Retired Title: Stop, you'll get better!

Number of meetings: 3 Cigarettes smoked before: 50 / day

> I had to get away from smoking at all costs; I knew that it could play a bad joke on me at any moment. The curiosity of entering a centre where they stop smoking was enormous: how could they be sure to master my vital instinct to light a cigarette using a methodology? I immediately put into practice all the tips in order to detoxify, relax and divert attention from the still near memory of the cigarette. Comparing some of my photos from two years ago with my image in the mirror now, you immediately notice that my body was too dry and my face sunken: I was not well at all and I didn't realize it. What I have done is effective, safe and useful to get back a healthy look and a lot of money to spend in a different way!

Dear smokers, without the toxic substances inhaled with the cigarette, your complexion will return to rosy: in this moment you are yellowish, be honest! Another testimony that I am very fond is Marc's one, a surgeon at Massachusetts Hospital. Start of meetings: January 31, 2005.

Name: Marc Age: 40 Profession: surgeon Title: I tried just to prove: It works!

> Already from the first meeting I did not feel any smoking stimulus, all right without smoking at all! After 10 days I perceived some stimulus (perhaps discomfort from having abandoned the cigarette), so thanks to the post-treatment check carried out with the operator and another meeting, I strengthened my wellness. After 5 months another meeting. Unconsciously after a few months, while I was traveling together with a friend, for fun (to smoke) I lit a cigar, and I was screwed! Thinking I could handle the matter in complete autonomy, I did not contact the support, I did not stop at that cigar, but I continued until I almost resumed. Despite this, I have not contacted the centre for help anymore and I can't tell you why. However, they have always specified to me: you contact us for any reason and when you wish. Something that may seem insignificant to you may be of great importance to us.

I had another session and so far, everything is great! I want and strongly desire this forever! Now it's up to me! It works, it's great! If you try... you can stop! If you just think about quitting ... I assure you that it will only remain a thought! I tried just to prove, and it works! Get started! Stop! Don't think about the cigarette anymore! Don't be afraid of getting fat or anything else, they are mostly stupid excuses. Like Frank and Marc, thousands of people have achieved their goal.

Many of them did not know or how to do it, they needed to be supported and they succeeded. Now, it's your turn!

3 THE PHASES OF THE JOURNEY

The smoke release process involves 4 stages. The first is the awareness one. Talking about health problems causes the smoker to get defensive. Confirm? It is useless to repeat sentences like "It gives you cancer", "You get intoxicated", "Smoking causes impotence" and all the others that you certainly know. Perhaps, it is more an outburst from the speaker than a threat to the smoker. However, the first step is to undermine, blow up the beliefs behind which the smoker hides, and introduce the appropriate reflection on the problem of smoking. Without attacking, but by making the smoker participate in the process and making him intervene in the first person. After all, the smoker knows he has a problem and, if put in the most suitable condition to be honest with himself, he will truly admit his problem, preparing to listen. On the contrary, if he is judged, it will be over.

Having understood, admitted the problem to oneself, what's next? The motivation is the following phase. Sometimes people tell me they understand that they do not have to and do not want to keep smoking, that it's stupid. But then, they continue to do it or stop the exercises. Why? Because they lack the energy, the propulsion to move forward, to commit themselves and continue to put the directions into practice despite the initial difficulties. Understanding is not enough; you need the right energy to make the leap in quality. It is essential to have strong *motivation* to act. There are many people who, when feel bad emotions, start smoking again. Do you think this is a coincidence? No, they have low energy. They retreat, returning to an earlier stage. And after finding the motivation, what follows? Action! Doing, doing and still doing something. Applying, applying, applying. Working on three aspects: mental, emotional, behavioural. And then the reconditioning to install a new wellness habit by eliminating the unhealthy and unproductive routines that revolve around the cigarette.

Description of the phases

Awareness is often confused with knowledge: they are not the same. Awareness will be characterized by a set of reasoning, arguments, different perspectives with respect to "clichés" and limiting beliefs about smoking, change, one's possibilities. In the *motivation* phase, you will learn how to create energy and lower the level of negativity, how to generate and maintain motivation. You will find out what stimulates you most towards well-being. In the *action* phase, on one hand, you will start doing new things that could prove to be very useful, on the other, you will detach yourself from others you were used to up to that moment. You will not always be persuaded of the goodness and effectiveness of what I will ask you to do: some things will seem strange, out of your reality: by doing them, you may feel stupid. I don't care. The essential thing is that they work by engaging you. If they are out of the ordinary, even better: it means they are better suited for a shift towards what you do not know. If they do not seem weird to you, it means that you already know them and that perhaps you have already tried them, but in vain. You must also be careful not to underestimate those recommendations which, although known and effective, are not always applied, or are carried out incorrectly, which is why you risk missing the object. And finally, through *reconditioning*, you will be able to create new and strong habits that will lead you to wellness. Therefore, you will have to repeat behaviours daily until you reach a certain degree of spontaneity.

What can happen

Often people stop after successfully passing the first stage. I must therefore warn you of an important aspect: if you do not complete all the phases of this path, awareness → motivation → action → reconditioning / well-being, you will return to the smokers' state. There is no middle ground. The cycle must be started and completed in order to pass to the next and higher level, to the condition of non-smokers. Those who do not create new habits, a new identity, suffer relapses by returning to the previous state. I know, I am paving the way for an apology: after all, a smoker can say that "I'm not capable" and "I'm not love myself so much" in order to continue smoking. Maybe you will have a relapse and feel lonely. You will tell yourself that after all the cigarettes was a company. Other smokers will tell you that it is a waste of time and all this "nonsense" is useless, or maybe that it only a question of *willpower*. Sentences that will only make you feel worse, because you will think you are nothing, without will. You will feel defeated thinking about how good it would be to smoke at least one. I must also prepare you for the idea that it will not always be easy to apply and daily suggestions, nor will it always be possible because you will be at work, or busy with your children, or with something else, or sometimes you just want to relax without doing anything or thinking about how to quit smoking. A bit like what happens to those who follow a diet and would like to eat what they are greedy for, at least for a day. But he also knows that by doing so, most likely, he would start gorging himself again and lose his job. And all would be lost.

Attention to self-sabotage thoughts!

A possible defensive reaction to the failure of expectations and result could bring you to think that:

1. It doesn't work with you and you can never stop.

2. The book doesn't work, it's useless.

3. It's all a joke.

4. Whoever wrote the book is a charlatan.

It is a characteristic form of resistance to change, a self-sabotage that instead of focusing attention on yourself, shifts it to something else. So, if any of these thoughts ever surface in your mind, do not give it weight: you already know it is not worth it. Instead, try to react with the following exercise that I propose to you.

Exercise

1. Stop negative thinking as if it were a photo.

Focus on the sentence, imagine the scene and relive the associated sensations as well.

2. Put your hand on your head and repeat, "Thank you for reminding me!"

3. Make the image disappear and turn it into your purpose with all possible details: sounds, colours, sensations. Focus on your goal and continue reading the book, being projected towards your wellness.

Other self-sabotage thoughts

- "If I stop, I will have other health problems, as happened to my father".

- "I don't believe in smoking cessation methods, even this one won't help much".

- "Maybe I can decrease to avoid possible damage".

- "Everything hurts even more than the cigarette and I can't help it".

- "I am not able, I am weak".

Beyond these situational "previews", do you know what is the best and most productive attitude? Relax deeply, take a deep breath and think that you decide, build, shape the result and achieve what you want.

You can do it

We will not rely on luck to free you from cigarettes. It will be the result of a strategy, a set of techniques and tools that have worked with thousands of smokers.

I will give you direct and indirect *suggestions*, which translated means "conditionings", "advices". The direct and particularly specific ones will serve you to intentionally implement a change, committing yourself to a desired result; the indirect ones will used to circumvent resistance to change.

In order to get the best results, I will ask you to perform exercises without explaining what they are for, to prepare the fertile ground for change. I will give you some practical suggestions, others - the most important - you will create yourself. You will be the one to identify the most useful and productive behaviours for each one. In fact, when a person elaborates the solution and puts it into practice autonomously, the change takes root because he has experienced the benefit that can derive from it.

If you feel the need to make an *inner change*, you already know that you want an improvement in quality. Do it now: create a structure of thoughts, emotions and actions that will lead you to the result.

I want you to reflect on another aspect in order to understand that you can change things: even smoking is a result! You usually get this because you think, feel emotions and behave in such a way as to be oriented towards the "cigarette": there is in fact a superficial structure with which we relate to the world and a deep one that conditions us, and we will change together. We will therefore work to "restructure" the cause that leads you to smoke, thus also acting on the result. It is important that you understand why you became a smoker. If the behaviour is only a symptom, an indicator, the real process of change will have to take place from the inside. Remember:

What has served you to be who you are is not useful for what you want to become!

If you follow my suggestions, something "magical" will happen you will unexpectedly quit smoking and get rid yourself from cigarettes forever! Without gaining weight, without discomfort, without problems, regaining great energy.

4 PREPARATION

A mistake that many smokers make is to define their degree of addiction based on clichés and learned beliefs. Evaluating how addicted you are to cigarettes is a very complex operation, often a double-edged sword. For this reason, I do not recommend defining yourself in this sense: avoid any kind of addiction test, it will not help you free yourself from smoking.

It is no coincidence that I have not included any in the book. First, we are too complex to be defined by the number of cigarettes smoked, or by the repetition of an appropriate gesture. Each of us has unique emotions, thoughts and personalities. If we believe that a high number of cigarettes smoked indicates a strong addiction, it would be a serious mistake. From personal experience, I can tell you that it was much easier to help people who could be defined as "heavy smokers" get rid of smoking than "habitual" non-smokers or "non-actual smokers". In fact, once a certain daily limit of cigarettes smoked is exceeded, there is a change of direction that depends on the smoker's degree of tolerance who, having reached this threshold, *realizes*, wakes up, feels the problem as concrete and thinks it is time *commit* to stop. It is your commitment that is needed.

Who smokes is not a weak person, this belief is *false*; indeed, you are *strong* if you can bear the smoke's weight? The fundamental question is that all this *energy* you use to endure the smoke cleaver, you could direct it towards health and wellness. Smokers have great power, but they turn it against themselves. One spring day - my favourite season - a few years ago, I was in my studio waiting for David, whom I had met for the first time three days earlier. David arrived on time. He entered the room assaulting me with a dazzling "Good-morning!", Enthusiastic about what he was about to do. He added: "You know I've almost quit smoking?!"

We had only had a first cognitive and motivational meeting. Nonetheless, David had the feeling that he was already cigarette free, just like so many other smokers I met. What had happened to him in the three days following our first meeting? The day we met, David had not come into my studio with a bright smile, on the contrary: he was tense and closed, on the defensive. I made him sit down and instantly he told me:

«I don't want to spend money; I don't want to quit smoking!»

> *If it is true that an unsolicited justification is an admission of guilt, this premise meant quite the opposite.*

The smoker who feels the need to defend himself without being attacked thus manifests the desire to get rid himself from the cigarette. It is a request for help: he does not know what and how to stop. By his way, David was also testing me. The smoker must feel he can trust, he tries to understand if he can really be helped and supported in the cessation process. Imagine yourself after quitting smoking. You have read everything and applied the tips literally, and you are finally free! Now suppose you meet a smoker you care about, and therefore want to motivate them to quit by setting your example. You explain to him how simple it was, even if challenging; you tell him that you did not think it was possible, yet you made it. You try to explain the concepts and transfer them to him, but the other remains entrenched in his own beliefs. You will understand what he is thinking: you have been smokers until sometime before too. You thought in the only way that protects cigarettes and not health too. With his sentence, «You know that I have almost stopped smoking?!», David confirmed to me that when the perception that "It is possible" creeps into people, when they see the concrete possibility of succeeding, an inner spring is triggered in them, and that is where the change begins. Before dismissing him, I said to David that day, "If you follow me to the letter, magic will happen. Yes, a real magic. Not everything has to have a rational explanation and be understood by the mind. You can afford to believe it and while you do it the change is already taking place, otherwise you wouldn't be here right now. Now relax and be receptive, here and now, take a deeper breath… all you feel, all you read is your new desire. You will be free to choose to be free very soon! ».

The idea of being a smoker

Change is generic. When you read "change", we mean "improvement" here. Many, on the other hand, replace one behaviour with a similar and sometimes more harmful one. Change is not always improvement.

Why does this happen? Because smoking is not an isolated aspect, but the result of a pattern of thoughts, emotions and actions that lead to the cigarette. In order to trigger the change, therefore, it is not enough to throw the pack of cigarettes in the bin, but you must work on this routine.

If, on the other hand, a person tries hard not to touch the cigarette, still having the idea of being a smoker ingrained in him, he is referring to the old method of willpower. He never stopped, because he is still a smoker inside. He may change the name on the document and call himself Mr. Hyde, but if he still feels like Dr. Jekyll, he will continue to be in this way, at least for himself. Smokers of this kind can try a thousand strategies and read all the books in the world: they will never stop. They may also change their beliefs and think that cigarettes are indeed the most harmful thing on Earth, but they will always remain frustrated smokers. Their identity is still that. Abstinence will only bring a period of discomfort, before resuming the cigarette in hand.

They will even be able to behave like convinced health-conscious people, play sports and follow a healthy diet and so on, but they will always be smokers, even without smoking. In fact, it is only by modifying the part of the identity connected to the cigarette that the change occurs spontaneously.

Change and improvement must take place in a person's depths, at the level of identity.

Password: growth!

Getting rid of smoking does not only consist in eliminating the cigarette, but it is also rather an inner change.

In fact, smoking is an automatic response that aims to bridge the gap between the current state you are in and the desired state you would like to be in.

People's malaise arises from the real or perceived inability to fill this gap. In the event of real disability, the person can always learn new skills and develop them to fill it.

If the inability is only perceived, you can work on your self-esteem, on self-confidence and in others. In both cases, there is always a concrete and useful solution for achieving one's goals. On the contrary, the cigarette is not a concrete and real way to do it, but only an apparent one. This explains the reason for the perennial smoker's dissatisfaction. Moving the addiction to cigarettes to another person, one thing or another behaviour, does not resolve the underlying malaise situation, it simply replaces one addiction with another.

Try to leave others out of this transformation process: you are the only one who can carry it out, it is all in your hands.

Do not rely on third parties: if you need support and seek "understanding", "care", "cuddles", you will not succeed, or you will get rest. It is important that this part of you grows. Growth! This is the password. Bet everything on you! Just beg for the affection and others' understanding! If it is true that smoking is the means by which the smoker asks for help and attention, a form of resistance against the path of liberation undertaken is precisely the search for attention from others. Growth requires a proactive and motivating environment, such as the one created having reached the goal. How would you feel smoke-free? In order to have the life you want? You must think and feel as if you have already achieved this purpose. Right now!

Try to answer those questions. Pause. Think about it.

They are used to make you reflect and direct your thoughts in the right direction. Quitting smoking is not a mathematical calculation; it is more of an alchemical formula, a personal magic potion that works thanks to you, only with you. In some ways it will be inexplicable, but it will happen.

Becoming free people

Orient your thinking in the most useful and powerful direction. Instead of quitting smoking, it is better to think about becoming a free person. Is not this idea more pleasant? There are people who quit smoking when they are happy. For example, a person who has met "love" feels happy and therefore is more likely to stop or otherwise decrease. However, it is likely that he has not actually quit, having simply replaced one form of addiction with another, or he is compensating for the addiction to smoking with the pleasure of falling in love. I'll explain. Love, like every other beautiful thing in life, in its healthy form is based on the principle of growth and freedom, not on the sacrifice one, suffering and limitation/imprisonment. Everything that allows you to grow is healthy, what limits it is not.

What limits does not make it grow. The cigarette is a prosthesis and if you leave it for another named "Phil", "Emily", "John", "alcohol", "heroin", etc., where is the growth? Attention, therefore, to the nature of the bonds we establish as we said at the beginning, growth is only possible in interdependence, in a system in which we feed ourselves, but, at the same time, leaves us free to evolve. I make the parallelism with the emotional relationship, because the concept of a two-person relationship is more understandable and closer to all of us. We often bond with people who mirror what we ourselves think of us, who confirm how we are inside. We approach "certain" people rather than others because they keep alive a game that we still insist on playing.

The nature of the bonds we establish depends only on us, on how we are, on the level of wellness achieved, on our degree of personal improvement. The more we become better people, the more we bring better people together. I do not want to offend your sensitivity by insinuating that maybe you are not as beautiful people as you think you are because you relate to cigarettes, or to the wrong people: I am not here to be nice to you, but to get you a concrete result. The reality is that if we are well and in balance with ourselves, if we are centred, stable inside, then we avoid what hurts us and we attract what improves us, makes us grow and feel good. This certainly does not include the cigarette.

Therefore we often delude ourselves into having quit smoking, when only the object of our addiction has changed. In order to be truly free, one must be independent and interdependent in relationships. The cigarette is that crutch that you are tempted to never leave, even after rehabilitation. The smoker does not know how to be alone and chooses the cigarette as "company". On the contrary, those who have learned to feel good about themselves not only avoid the harmful relationship with the cigarette, but also have the possibility of establishing new relationships in a perspective of well-being.

The broken leg

Let's continue with the image of the crutch. After months of plastering, go to the doctor; he visits you, confirms that everything went well and that the bones have calcified in the correct position. Once the plaster is removed, you begin to feel lighter and take a few shy steps with the aid of the crutch. Little by little, place your foot on the ground increasingly more markedly, even if you fear the pain. After a certain period of testing, thanks to the results that gradually give you more confidence, you begin to unload more weight on the recovering leg and to lean less on the crutch; in short, you are surer of yourself. You are finally free and throw the crutch forever. A few months later you find yourself again playing soccer matches with friends, jogging or practicing your favourite sport. In a completely spontaneous way, you take back your life as it always has been. Do not think about the crutch anymore, nor about the fear that accompanied it: everything happened naturally. The rehabilitation from the crutch took place thanks to your commitment and the doctors' guidance. You did not doubt the result, or the doctors; you trusted them, because they are experts. If you did not, you would not be able to walk anymore. What complicates the process of releasing the cigarette compared to the crutch's example is the "non-visibility" of the result, based only on a sensation. Just as walking you feel with certainty that the leg is healing, by breathing deeply you will have the certainty of freedom from the cigarette. The change, if deeply desired, occurs in the absence of resistance, in a spontaneous and natural way.

Reconditioning towards wellness

There is no set time within which I promise you the desired change. There is only the time of your personal journey, during which you will have to carry out what I ask of you and return if the result is late in coming. Like a champion who fails to repeat the known and desired result he tries again, again and again until victory, because he knows that he has already been there, that he can return and will come back. Yes, because objective time, which is only a concept, does not exist. Sometimes he is a good travel companion, sometimes an enemy. The most important time *is your time*, what you have inside. Respect for yourself.

While reading the book, I will be always next to you, holding your hand, accepting your request for support and I will not be afraid to yell in your ears with a nice megaphone to instil confidence! Whenever you say, "I can't do it", my voice will awaken you, amplified by a red megaphone placed near your favourite ear. In that moment, an emotion, a great energy will invade your body, and spontaneously you will hear these words echoing in your head, as your fist will become tighter, and you will say to yourself: "Yes, I can do it!", "I am greater than any difficulty!", "I face everything!" (repeat it now). Right now, right in these lines, we have a great confirmation... you want change! Rest assured, we are on the right path. Think about your wellness, and do not worry about others, at least in our path. The most important people for me are you! Read, meditate and relax your mind, listen to your feelings. A few days and the work done will begin to sprout. Make sure you are the most important person to you now!

5 AWARENESS

«*It is always an emotion*

observe a world you know well

from a new perspective».

Bill Bryson

John, 54, after quitting smoking said to me: «I finally understand!».

Me: «What? ». J: «Only now I'm thinking about living my life. Before, I tried to live a life that did not belong to me, made up of prejudices, labels, false certainties and I was increasingly distancing myself from myself».

Me: «What do you mean? » J: «I hid all my weaknesses and insecurities. I made everyone believe that I was strong, that I was well, that I was right, and I was happy. Inside of me, however, I was often dissatisfied, I had the perpetual feeling of emptiness. Whatever I did, I avoided feeling bad, I avoided facing that indefinite something that could destabilize my certainties. Whatever I did was aimed at confirming what I already thought, the idea I had made of myself and others; but I didn't respect myself. I felt that something was wrong, but I deliberately ignored my discomfort».

Me: «How do you know? » J: «I have always sought my satisfaction in relationships, in work, in everything, even in sport. After doing the meetings and exercises with you, I started to see my situation from other perspectives».

Me: «What did you see? » J: «That of everything I did and did there was nothing that reflected what was important to me at that moment! »

Me: «Let me understand better...». J: «I followed my parents' wishes, even if I recognized them as "right" from an objective point of view, I didn't feel them right for me at that moment. Like a nice dress, but in a different size. I liked the dress a lot, but the size was too tight for me. I grew up and clothes as a little boy did not fit me anymore. Now I have renewed the wardrobe! ».

Me: «Tell me about the new wardrobe.» J: «Now I count, I live my life!».

Me: «How do you understand that you are living your life? » J: «From now on I do everything that gives me a sense of fullness and satisfaction before, during and after. Without guilt. I am important. That's why I started smoking and why I continued, why I felt empty».

Me: «What do you mean? » J: «My inner dissatisfaction, not being listened to led me to seek that lack of feeling of fullness in something else.

At the age of 13 I weighed 80 kg; I was fat. I had found in food the possibility to fill myself with something, but afterwards I always had a feeling of emptiness inside. Then, I started smoking, and it seemed to give me "something", but immediately after the total emptiness. So, do romantic relationships, work, fun. I started things and they always left me with a sense of dissatisfaction. I never stopped looking for fullness, but I always found emptiness. In order to answer the question above: now I follow the fullness, I feel it. If after an experience I feel the sad feeling of emptiness, I avoid repeating it. As I finally did with the cigarette. In fact, I started playing sports and following a hobby I had as a child and this gives me great pleasure and satisfaction. I'm living my life, I feel it ». The smoker seeks satisfaction in smoking that has its roots elsewhere. Only after admitting it to himself was John able to get rid of the cigarette. He understood, he became more aware and changed his attitude, learning to really listen to himself and to enjoy his life. Do you say it is not possible? So, keep on smoking, to live the life you lead! You are at a crossroads: either continue with your apology, or change.

A decision to make

In the first moments when you start smoking, and for some subsequent period, you experience the repetition of the gesture in a mechanical way. Gradually it will become a habit, which will then lead to addiction. I remember Margaret repeating to me: «I can't help it. I like it. I miss. It wasn't like that before. It bothered me. It stank and made me sick. Today it doesn't suck, and I like it. I love the taste. And to think that at first I was nauseated... and undeterred I continued to be accepted by others! » All the smokers I have met have told me that their first cigarette really sucked. It made them sick and annoyed especially by the stench it left on them. Yet each of them has found a *good reason* to continue. If the use of the cigarette is limited and mechanical, it is not pleasant; become automatic, it begins to please and to strengthen itself to the point of abuse. The vital energy, the gift received at birth, is reduced ("This is not done", "Do not move", "This is right because I say so", "It is not possible because the system does not allow it", etc. .). The Great Child that was in you is small today. Energy is low.

Low energy = Low opinion of self = Dependence

Hear these words that I am saying to you as if I were standing in front of you: (Write your name and read) ....**Karen**............................, *I warn you that it will not be easy, even if they are simple steps to follow. It will be a job in which we both can and must commit ourselves, a job to do together. It will not always be so unpleasant, indeed: at times, you will even find it funny. But remember that there may be moments of despair... otherwise the satisfaction of having made it where would it be? Well, we are on the right path!*

As you read these pages, I will stay with you, you will never be alone: this dialogue will generate a new voice within you, which will become your internal supervisor and will always accompany you. If you are wondering: «When do you make me quit smoking? », The answer is: «We have already started! ». Before continuing and closing the circle around you, before starting to be yourself without any "prosthesis" - yes, because the cigarette is a prosthesis - it is essential, however, that you decide! But do not get me wrong: I do not mean the big decision; you do not have to quit smoking right now. For the moment, I am referring to another decision: to keep reading the book with conviction following all the suggestions.

Margaret admitted that she still felt deeply torn, after a series of meetings. On the one hand, she wanted to quit smoking because she felt that she was not doing her good, on the other hand the idea of continuing with her consultations seemed to her to be all wasted effort, especially in those moments when everything else went wrong. She confided to me that a couple of days earlier she had been tempted to call me to erase our appointment. However, she eventually showed up because she felt the desire to change things.

«You are at a crossroads, Margaret» I told her, «you have to make a decision: stop and live your usual life or continue with the meetings. But remember one thing: if you stop now, it would be like admitting to yourself that you can't, that a simple cigarette is bigger and stronger than you. This also means that you can never find out what our journey together would reveal to you in the short term and change your life for the better. If you decide to continue, congratulations! It means that you are foolish and brave enough to question your "stability". However, a great reward awaits you: freedom! ». Now it's your turn to make the same decision: do you want to stop and continue with your usual life or take the risk and change the rules of the game?

But before moving on, I want you to dwell on what Johann Hari[6] wrote about addiction:

> «In the 1970s, a psychology professor in Vancouver named Bruce Alexander noticed something odd about this experiment. The mouse is placed in a cage by itself. He has nothing to do but administer the drugs. What would happen then, he wondered, if we set it differently?

So, Professor Alexander built a "mouse park". A luxury cage inside which the mice would have had coloured balls, the best food for rodents, tunnels in which pawkings and many friends: everything a metropolitan mouse could aspire to. What would happen then, Alexander wondered?

In the "mouse park" everyone obviously ended up tasting the water from both bottles, not knowing what was inside. However, what happened next was surprising. The mice who lived a good life did not like drugged water. They mostly avoided it, consuming less than a quarter than isolated mice. None of them died. And while all the mice kept alone and unhappy made heavy use of it, this did not happen to any of those immersed in a happy environment». Professor Alexander's study suggests that when we are in a state of psychophysical wellness, we are inclined to stay there and consolidate it, avoiding malaise and addiction. Conversely, we often cradle or resign ourselves in unhealthy and uncomfortable situations, thus predisposing us to addiction, which begins to attract and like us. But, when we feel well-being and happiness, we enjoy the true flavour of life, and nothing else can be so good, not even the infamous cigarette. I say and repeat it: you are not only here to quit smoking, but you are also here to become a better person!

Where are you

In the diagram below it is represented the moment of your birth, with a line that projects towards the future. When you were born you were at your full potential and your most powerful energy. Suddenly, everything you had to stay in the world was no longer enough and you added something: the cigarette prosthesis. The cigarette is a tribal rite, an initiation that marks the transition to the adult

---

[6] J. Hari, op. cit.

world, a sort of preferential lane that accelerates the maturation process, acts as a certificate of passing the final exams. Who are the examiners? The others. You therefore smoke to prove to others that he is a strong and independent adult. Nowadays, we know with certainty that the opposite is true. In your life line, at a specific point, you have taken a detour. You have continued along this parallel path for all these years until today; maybe, sometimes, you have returned to the road of origin, but then you have preferred the detour.

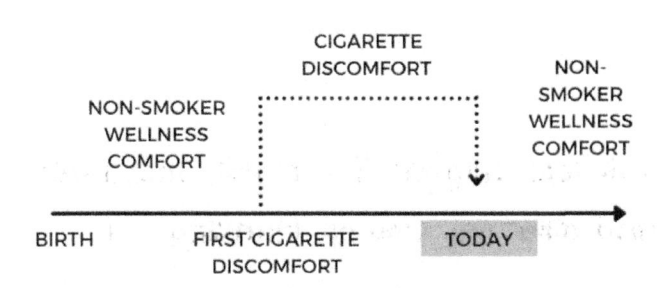

```
                    CIGARETTE
                    DISCOMFORT         NON-
                   ·················   SMOKER
   NON-SMOKER      :              :    WELLNESS
   WELLNESS        :              :    COMFORT
   COMFORT         :              :
                   :              ↓
   ─────────────────────────────────────►
   BIRTH          FIRST CIGARETTE    TODAY
                   DISCOMFORT
```

It is important to understand that real life is only on the starting path.

Exercise

Take a deep breath and feel yourself back on the original path. You are finally free!

Press the thumb and forefinger of your right hand (PIDX) and repeat aloud: "I am a free person!". Come on, don't smile!

Do it.

Tell me about you

Do you want to continue smoking? Or do you want to be free? If you feel confused, make your decision only after reading the book and putting into practice everything it advices. "The fear of giving up doing something, of taking risks by leaving what we know and changing things is inherent in all of us". I tried to explain to Margaret when she confided her uncertainty. "However, there comes a time when you realize that you can no longer go on as you always have, that you need to change course, that you have to take the risk because there is a higher stake." The same is for you.

What pushed you to be here, to hold this book in your hands and read it?

I am scared that I will become unwell. My breathing is noticeably getting worse, I always feel tired and sluggish. I can't afford it

Well, why are you reading this?

I hope it will trigger the right mindset in me and alter my way of thinking. I don't seem to be able to do it on my own.

What do you mean? Explain better.

I just don't seem to be able to alter my thinking on my own. Even though I am worried it doesn't seem to be enough

Well, ultimately are you reading this because...?

I want to stop smoking - before it kills me.

It seems like the same question repeated, I know. But it is not. Or rather, it is partly in order to elaborate a more useful to you answer.

> I'll give you an example:
>
> Why are you reading this book?
>
> *Because they recommended it to me.*
>
> What do you mean? Explain better...
>
> *Because I smoke and I would like to quit. I have tried many times in vain.*
>
> Well, ultimately are reading you this because...?
>
> *I want to get rid of the cigarette forever!*

I don't want to condition your answer with this example. I have included it just to make it clearer that, when we answer a question, we are unlikely to be honest at the first answer, especially with ourselves and if the topic is to quit smoking. But usually, after three questions, the true and profound motivation comes out, without excuses or resistance, or in any case you get close to the truth. I want you to be honest with yourself. Write down what you feel, what and how you would like it to be.

What would you *want* to happen reading this book?

I would like to learn to value myself.
To stop smoking because I have no need
or desire to and to feel so much better.

Now, that you have given the answer, convince me that what you have written is true, that it is useful to you. What are the reasons for your answer?

> I'll give you an example:
>
> *I want to get rid of the cigarette forever. I am tired from all the times I have tried to in vain, and I feel unmotivated.*
>
> *I would like to be free from the cigarette and I would like to succeed this time.*
>
> What motivations support this goal of yours?
>
> - I have erection problems.
> - I am not a good example for my children.
> - I spend too much.
> - I want to improve my fitness.
> - ...

Answer:

I am fed up of being scared that I will die. Off constantly feeling rubbish and ashamed and dissapointed in myself for starting to smoke again

List of reasons in support of the answer:

I am fat, ugly & just hate myself.
I want to improve my fitness and be able to exercise & lose weight.
I want to stop washing money — I can't afford it or jushfy it.
I want to value myself.
I really don't like myself or care enough about what happens. Deep down I blame myself for Poul's death.

Now, for each of the reasons you have filled in, be specific and expand what you have written by asking yourself the "reason why".

> Example: *I am not a good example for my children.*
>
> Why? What are the behaviours, thoughts and emotions that make you say this?
>
> *I feel guilty when I say that in life you must be strong and committed, while I am feeling weak and incapable, without willpower!*

This is just an example, it may not concern you, but you certainly also have good reasons and contradictions in terms of values. The more the motivations are specific and oriented towards a positive dimension, the more powerful, constructive and closer they are to our deepest values. Instinctively answer the questions I ask you: the more often you think, the worse it is. Put your stomach and heart in front of reasoning. The answers will serve as a map to better orient you in the depths of your mind. Write as much as you can. The clearer and more detailed you are, the sooner you free yourself.

Be a smoker or not

Smoking, as well as using drugs or alcohol, arises from a mix of needs: the first of *personal and social affirmation* and the other as a *request for care*. These seemingly antithetical aspects are instead closely related: those who suffer from addiction, in general, do not feel recognized for what they think they are or deserve.

If I had to tell you all the cases I have encountered and which confirm this aspect, it would take a whole book. I will limit myself to mentioning one that struck me in a particular way. It is Adele's story, a middle-aged lady, an affectionate and "helpful" wife of a husband who is often ungrateful, who never valued her work. The more she felt neglected, the more she sought the attentions of her husband, to be seen and considered not only as a wife but also as a woman. Adele did even more with her children, but her boys, although they appreciated what their mother did for them, took it for granted; thanks, on their part, was not contemplated. Despite her great dedication, Adele was therefore not seen by her family as she wished, and this pushed her to commit herself beyond measure, to the point of putting herself aside. Adele seemed to live according to her family, and the more her request for attention and recognition fell on deaf ears, the more her number of cigarettes smoked increased, starting to cause her health problems. There are not a few people who react like this in similar situations.

However, realizing that the problem was growing and fearing that it would become increasingly more serious over time, Adele took courage and showed up in my office. "I'm afraid that if I continue like this, I'll have more and more trouble... and what will I do with my husband and the boys?" was the first thing she said to me, all alarmed. The questions you find below are the same ones I asked her when, during the interviews, Adele realized that her addiction was somehow linked to the family dynamics that had arisen. Here is what I asked her:

What are you worried about the current situation?

That I will become more and more unhealthy, until I do so much harm I will get a serious illness

Did you have any difficulties / problems with the cigarette?

makes me cough and feel tired, lacking in energy.

What difficulties/problems might you have in the future by continuing to smoke?

My breathing and health will continue to deteriate and I will get cancer / COPT.

Are you worried about all this? How do you live the present considering these problems?

Becoming increasingly more worried and beginning to feel the effects more on my breathing and health.

How would you be different today if you never smoked?

I would be healthier, wealthier and more confident in myself. I feel weak having to rely on smoking.

How and in what could you be different tomorrow by freeing yourself from the cigarette today?

I would be more energised, healthier, free! more able to exercise. I would feel proud of myself. I wouldn't smell disgusting all the time. I hate the taste afterwards in my mouth.

What makes you want to keep smoking?

I depend on it. I feel it relaxes me. When I get low/sad I rely on them. I know it doesn't help but somehow can't free myself of it.

The 7 reasons why you keep going

The reasons why a smoker does not quit can fall into one or more of the following categories:

1. Low self-esteem. He does not believe in himself and/or thinks he cannot make it.

"I'll never make it, it's stronger than me! I'm not capable of it"

it seems to be his motto. This attitude can extend to other aspects of the smoker's life, of which the cigarette is a spy, a signal.

2. Self-harm. He does not love himself; he does not feel deserving. He has a strong anger towards someone, but not being able to express it towards the outside, he turns it against himself. "I started smoking to hurt my father," one of my clients once told me. «It was a way to get his attention, after the breakup he never really cared much about us. He didn't give a damn anyway. Actually, it was me the only one who have lost! ».

[handwritten margin note: Hate myself Caused Paul's illness.]

3. Sense of captivity. It is common in long-time smokers, now accustomed to the deprivation of personal freedom: "That's how it is now, what do you want to change at forty/fifty/sixty years old? We might as well continue, what's done is done!"

[handwritten margin note: Done harm now anyway.]

4. Feeling of loss of sense. The cigarette has become the frame of the life picture, without which life would not have the same sense. «I'm afraid I won't make it, it's as if without a cigarette I was unable to do everything I did before. The cigarette is my life partner », one of my clients confided to me once.

5. Lack of skills/help. He does not know what and how to stop. "I would like to, but I don't know where to start.

I've read something here and there but I'm the classic person who throws in the towel without someone to guide him" is one of the sentences I have heard more often by people who have just entered my studio.

6. Low energy. He is not motivated enough (motivation is the force that brings you closer to "pleasure" and away from "pain"):

"But even if I tried, what would it change?" "What does assure me I'd be better off? What do you think I could do in my situation...?"

7. Lack of a clear purpose. This kind of smoker has no attractive goals in life. «What good would it do? It doesn't change my life. It's already bad now, let alone without it... And in any case, it wouldn't be the cigarette that made the difference», one of my first clients told me, who came to the interview at the insistence of a friend who had already stopped smoking. Following a very troubled period in the sentimental and working fields, Massimo had entered a condition of heavy smoking and apathy. It took him a while to understand that he needed to break away from the past and redesign his life starting from himself, without settling for the "crutch" of smoking.

In fact, all smokers want to quit smoking. They know and feel that quitting is important to live better. However, in some cases, it is appropriate to strengthen the *motivation* that can support the change, the inner drive that allows you to reach the desired and empowering status, in order to move away from a painful and limiting situation. Why is it necessary to reinforce motivation?

It often happens that as a child one is limited in dreams or dissuaded from the idea of reaching wellness goals or pursuing one's ambitions. Thus, we are convinced that it is not possible or that we are not capable. Psychologists call this mechanism "learned helplessness". It is precisely in this "impossibility" that addiction ferments.

How would you like your health and wellness to be?

I would love to feel energised, feel good again. Able to regain fitness, motivated to lose weight and feel good. I have forgotten how that feels.

What should you do to achieve this ideal condition?

Stop smoking, cut back on drinking, eat healthier. Start to exercise.

What should you avoid instead?

> *All of the above.*
> *I seem to be on a mission to destroy myself and I don't really know why. At the same time I do also want to change but keep putting obstacles in my way.*

Visualize the images of that ideal state within yourself and always keep them in mind. Place them in front of you, so that they always remind you of the goal you are aiming for. Zoom them in and hang them on the walls of your mind.

Others quit on their own

All smokers would like to be among "those able to quit on their own". In fact, there are cases of voluntary cessation in which with commitment and choice it is possible to quit, and others of spontaneous cessation: suddenly, smoking is not part of one's ways of doing and being. In the latter case, I am referring to those smokers who one day, for no apparent reason, or perhaps for a coincidence that made them think a little more than usual, throw the pack of cigarettes in the bin.

Be very careful! There are very few who experiences this evet. If you think there are many you are wrong, it is not the rule. It becomes known because there is open talk of spontaneous cessation, which is an obvious fact. Those who fail do not boast about it, no one notices it. There are many more *failures*. Those who resume smoking often feel ashamed and do not talk about it so easily. Cases of *spontaneous remission* are a bit like those incurable diseases that disappear in an inexplicable way for the doctors themselves. Everything has an explanation, even if for the moment science has not found an answer yet. If a change occurs, it means that something has changed inside the individual, albeit in an unconscious way.

Based on decades of experience with my clients, I can say instead that a good 95% of smokers take a more tortuous path, which goes from indifference, to the idea of getting rid of cigarettes, in order to "I have to quit". Sometimes from indifference to "I must". By indifference I mean what Di Clemente and Prochaska define as "pre-contemplation of the change's stages"7, a phase in which a person does not think at all about giving up smoking, not because the difficulties are deliberately ignored, but because in this phase the difficulties they do not exist at all in the smoker's mind, they are not considered in the least.

In the life path with the cigarette, the smoker creates a parallel reality of "fake wellness". However, a serious reason why he must think about it sooner or later comes. For example, a disease (cancer, heart attack, emphysema or even reduced sexual performance, exhaustion, breathlessness, nocturnal dyspnoea, etc.) And he finds himself forced to quit for his health. Otherwise, despite the damage to his health, he fails. Such is the difficulty that he prefers to repeat to himself and to reiterate to others that he likes to smoke or that he is unable to quit. Today we know that this is not the case, it is a defence mechanism. No one likes coercion, no one perceives the ban in a positive way and the ban itself is, maybe, one of the "good reasons" why the smoker has become what he is. Follow my reasoning. The cigarette can take on the function of a means of self-affirmation:

"I do what I want", it means to go against the imposed prohibitions.

Smoking arises from a ban. Are you in?

The interesting aspect is that, in this vicious circle, the smoker often becomes a smoker to counter a *ban*, ending up creating one himself: or rather, he is forbidden to touch the cigarette for his own well-being. Smoking arises from a ban and returns to it.

It's a repurposed pattern, a dog chasing its own tail. Paul McKenna, world-famous hypnotherapist I got to know personally, in his book Quit Smoking Today: Without Gaining Weight[8] reports the story told by Robert Hughes in *The Fatal Shore*, where it is said that Australian prisoners in the English colonies were willing to be whipped and deprived of food and water in order to smoke tobacco and drink rum.

---

[7] C.C. Di Clemente, J.O. Prochaska, "Self-change and therapy change of smoking behaviors: A comparison of processes of change of cessation and maintenance", « Addictive Behaviors», 1982, 7, pp. 133-142.

[8] P. McKenna, Quit Smoking Today: Without Gaining Weight, Sterling; Har/Com edition (May 5, 2016).

Deprivation and prohibition increase the value of the object, and of clandestine behaviour.

The deprivation's object becomes fascinating and desired. For the prisoners, smoking and drinking was a manifestation of freedom, it meant affirming one's identity despite the consequences (the whip). Similarly, the tie with the cigarette increasingly anchors the principle of deprivation/prohibition to the meaning of freedom. Just as the prisoners in the English colonies of the nineteenth century passed from one *prison* to another (the cigarette), even the smoker, in order to escape to his "psychological cell", takes refuge behind the bars of the "cigarette". Smoking is linked to the sense of freedom and, at the same time, it is a manifestation of imprisonment. Smoking gives the feeling of being able to decide and exercise control, when it is just a dysfunctional mechanism. It is the cigarette that manages you, and not the other way. In situations of freedom deprivation, attachment to cigarettes increases.

But you now can consciously choose to free yourself. You decide this time, not the cigarette. You are not forced by a sudden malaise, by an event external to your will, you do not "have to do it". From indifference, you are now in a phase of interest; go further, move on to "I can stop", "I can free myself now" and from there, to "I want to stop" and "I do it": with serenity, commitment, effectiveness and forever. You can do it, each according to your own times: meditate with me on what and how; work on yourself, on your potential. This time it will be different and unprecedented because you will be the one to choose. The power is in your hands!

A question of identity

Whoever truly eliminates cigarettes from his life is not a former smoker, but a non-smoker. The difference is very deep. What's your name? What if instead of calling you by name they recognized you as the so and so's ex, with whom you had a relationship in the past? Or like the son of a well-known and bulky father? How would you feel? It would not be nice. Do you know why? Our identity is not touched, and it is not exchanged. The function of identity is to recognize oneself. Each of us has their own identity card and just look at the photo, read their name, we can recognize that we are that person, sometimes a little younger, but still us. Moreover, identity is used to make us recognized by others. Our identity defines us, it belongs to us deeply. Thanks to her meetings, Adele had the opportunity to reflect and finally become aware of her *status* as a smoker. Not only that, but she also understood that the fundamental problem lay not in her behaviour, but in her way of being and perceiving herself in relation to her husband and children.

The questions you find below helped Adele to focus on her opinion about herself up to the moment she decided to change. I'm sure answering will help you too.

How do you associate the cigarette with your identity?

I feel as if I am weak, lacking in willpower. Having to rely on a cigerette to function when others manage without.

How do others see you?

Soft, a push over. Someone who has alot of additions and not strong. They laugh at me and think I am not capable.

How would you like to be seen?

Strong, independent. Healthy, fit. Able to cope with life. Not someone to take the piss out of.

Answer the questions honestly: the answers you give provide a framework for your relationship with the cigarette. Already feel for how you would like to be seen by others. In order to become oneself, at times, a person must "pretend" to be that individual. You should be who and how you would like to be. I know it may seem simplistic and reductive. This is not the case at all: the thought focused on the idea you have of yourself has determined your life up to this day. So, from now on, orient your thoughts on "who" you would like to be and "how" you would like your life to be. If by imagining your future, you see yourself in negative conditions, change your image. Make it beautiful, pleasant and attractive.

If you had the power and willingness to be who you want, who would you want to become?

Someone who stands up for themselves. Is confident. Who is proud of who they are and what they have acheived.

Healthy, slim, energetic, no longer a people pleaser. Say no more. Is who I want to be, not what I think people want me to be. Strong.

> Answer the question: How would I like to be?
>
> Start responding in a way that push you to get the best result.
>
> Take a blank sheet of paper and write in different colours using the space as you wish. Use adjectives to define who and how you will be and feel.
>
> For example, a student wrote a nice "big" in the centre in red. Then, "entrepreneur, rich, happy, father, athletic, handsome, attractive, charismatic", and he hung the paper in his room, right in front of the bed, in order to see it first thing in the morning as soon as he woke up, and lastly evening before falling asleep. I don't know what and how he pictured all this in his mind, it doesn't matter; what matters is that looking at the paper every day strengthened in that man the meaning attributed to the words and the associated emotions. You can place the sheet somewhere in your office or set it as a background on your PC or mobile phone. Organize yourself as you prefer. Play this "game" from now on and in a few weeks, you will see the results!

The 3 identities

The three identities are:

1. Smoker.

2. Former smoker.

3. Non-smoker.

You know the first one very well. Even the second one, and to be precise it is the kind of smoker who "falls back", who still thinks about the cigarette, who still wants to smoke a cigarette, who tries hard not to smoke and occasionally sniffs one in memory of the old glorious days and relies on the famous "willpower", which does little work. Probably some of you have already stopped and started again. The third identity is our goal: to become non-smokers, better people. Just to be clear, I'll give an example: the first identity is that if they call "Phil", you turn around and answer because it's you. In the case of the second identity, however, you are still Phil, but to avoid contact you refrain from turning around.

They call you; you know they refer to you, you do not turn around yet. You want to prove that you are another person. The last case is when they call you Phil and you do not turn around, because your name is Felice.

You are *really* another person.

Quitting smoking: a sacrifice or a commitment?

Willpower

Contrary to popular belief, willpower can do little when it comes to quitting smoking. Let me explain why. Sooner or later we all experience moments of great fatigue, which involve a lot of effort for us. In such periods, what keeps us going and tackling the climb is willpower. These moments are not negative, on the contrary, they often serve to grow, they are a means to obtain a good result. In fact, when we are pressured to achieve a goal, we focus better and deliver results.

The important thing is that these periods of fatigue last a limited time, have a beginning and an end. The drawbacks arise from the "willpower" applied to the bitter end, which turns into an obsession to achieve a goal. Like someone who wants to lose weight by striving to put into practice diets that never work, because they tend to implement obsessive control. According to a research commissioned by the American Psychologist Association and lasting 18 years, about 80% of the dieters interviewed were overweight, while 70% of those who did not follow the diet were of normal weight[9]. It is therefore deduced that

---

[9] G. Nardone, *Psicotrappole*, Ponte alle Grazie, 2013 Milan, pp. 104-111.

dieting makes you fat. Controlling nutrition, depriving oneself, exercising obsessive control, in fact, worsens the situation.

On the contrary, learning to better organize meals and eating some "forbidden" foods in certain ways and times helps losing weight faster and maintaining the achieved weight over time. Without "effort" but investing one's commitment in creating new habits. The same happens with smoking: the more you want to control it, the more willpower you put into it, the more you lose control and the more you smoke. For this reason, take a new and empowering perspective instead of trying not to smoke start managing and organizing cessation by following the directions and according to what you think is most suitable for you. Imagine "willpower" as a dam: the more you insist, the more the basin fills and the more it creates pressure, to the point that the banks, due to excessive tension, risk breaking. And if it happens - you know what I mean - anger, guilt and frustration come out, devastating what you built and leaving you with the feeling of having lost everything and the desperation of having to start all over again. This is what happens when "willpower" is applied without knowing what and how to do: everything becomes useless endurance. Willpower can also play an important role in initiating choice, but motivation also needs to take over. Remember that willpower is an effort that must last for a limited time and motivation does not last forever. So, they are both useful, but not decisive. What is needed is commitment. It is therefore a combination of factors.

The commitment

Imagine pushing a car to its destination. How many meters could you travel by dragging the car with your own strength? 100 meters? 500 meters? You could not make it any further. This is willpower. The commitment, on the other hand, is to push the car with a driver who knows how to start. The effort is limited to that event, soaked in the sweat of awareness and the knowledge and skills necessary to start the engine. And if the car does not start, you could always call the tow truck or a mechanic, in short, asking for help. The psychology of commitment does not generate the sense of guilt and renunciation typical of the incorrect consideration and willpower's application. In fact, as useful as it is, willpower cannot be enough alone: method and strategy are needed. Otherwise, your mind will end up obsessing with the result without adequately focusing the task: discipline, organization and resource management are required. What I ask you is a good dose of commitment in order to follow the suggestions without prejudice and in total freedom. It is not so much a question of willpower, but rather of the desire to achieve improvement, to dedicate oneself to what makes you feel good, to do what will bring long-term benefits despite the initial difficulties and reluctances. So, I am not referring to a change with immediate effects, but to the result of a journey. Instead, a common problem is that people try to get everything immediately and, by doing so, they do not give themselves the time to implement new behaviours, perhaps more difficult than usual, but which could lead them to change. They continue to repeat consolidated patterns, which obviously cannot lead them to anything new. Just to be even clearer, imagine going to the gym: you must work hard to achieve concrete and measurable goals, to get the desired shape, which you will certainly not gain after just one afternoon of activity, but following a period of constant training. Commitment comes from an interest, a passion, a goal, a purpose. Otherwise, willpower intervenes when you are in the gym and you must push the muscles beyond their standard, in order to perform a particularly demanding and challenging exercise. If at that moment you are not at the top, but you know you still must train, use your willpower to tackle the required exercise. This is a definite circumstance. Wellness will be the natural consequence, therefore, not so much of a constant sacrifice, to be carried out every day with willpower, just like a determined commitment that turns into habit. So focus your attention on who you would like to become and how you would like to be.

We are predisposed to the news

Smoking is not only a form of physical addiction that involves nicotinic receptors, but also involves changes in the neurological structure of the brain. Every day, the central nervous system undergoes changes. We are our neurological structure. As demonstrated by the brain studies conducted by Dr. Dispenza[10], it is possible to remodel one's neurological circuits by changing thoughts and emotions with commitment and knowledge. Our work together will therefore be focused on the elimination of physical dependence (15-30 gg) and the creation of a new empowering neurological structure. Recent discoveries in the neurological field tell us that every 3 seconds our brain asks itself: "What's new?" So:

"1, 2, 3: what's new?", "You are a free person!" Our brain expects us to do something different in order to learn new strategies, patterns and habits. In other words, the brain is programmed for change. We are the ones who give the direction towards "worsening" or "improvement". We can change our neurological structure at any time. Would you like to know the technique to modify your neurological structure and orient yourself towards improvement?

---

[10] Dispenza, Evolve Your Brain: The Science of Changing Your Mind, Health Communications Inc, 2008.

I'm about to tell you what to do, but are you willing to do it? It is much simpler and easier than you might think, however you must be consistent. You are ready? Are you willing to start now and continue for 10 minutes a day until your goal is achieved?

Good! Simply start imagining who you would like to be and how you would like your life. Imagine how you would like to be in a year. Experience the scene as if it were happening now. Do this every day for 10 minutes. Choose to be who you will be. Get started!

The smoker's resistances and the "dictatorship of habits"

Smokers who cannot quit do not really want to; they do not want to change. Let's see a rundown of their most typical behaviours. Who do you recognize yourself in?

- The Prophet. He is that smoker who after trying several times closes himself in his armour, putting his life back in the hands of "destiny".

- The Cry-baby. He tries in vain to quit and then justifies himself by saying that he does not find support and understanding from family and friends; or he does not start at all, with the excuse of not having support or other alleged difficulties.

- The Repentant. He is willing to say that he is weak rather than striving to change and free himself from smoking. Addiction can get people to say things you would not say in other circumstances!

Someone might also think thoughts like: "If I could, I would have done it already!", "It is easy for him who is not in my situation", "My life is so heavy that I do not wish it to anyone, how do I do it?", "I try but everything is always against me", etc. Life is in your hands! Nobody can influence you if you do not allow it. If you do not dedicate time to your well-being and always put others, children, friends in front of you, then you will be unhappy, you will feel anger, sadness and frustration. You are the most important people! If you give yourself permission to be happy despite everything, to enjoy life and build the future you want, then everyone around you will benefit. Each of us goes through difficulties in life. I am aware that it is not easy to change and improve things. Sometimes, despite the commitment, it seems impossible. However, only you can do it, and no one can act for you. In order to free yourself from cigarettes, it is essential that you understand why and how you developed this habit, with all that it entails (thoughts, emotions, behaviours). It is not the only step, however it is crucial, and, for this reason, we will come back several times, to work on those mechanisms that make the cigarette your tyrant. Let me explain at first, you did not know how to smoke, but you have learned. You took the cigarette and tried to smoke it, then slowly you got used to it and from a simple mechanical act it became "natural". Perhaps you are among those smokers who cannot wait to go home and sit on the balcony with the inevitable glass of wine and a cigarette to enjoy the well-deserved relaxation at the end of the day too. Or among those who go to the bar not for coffee but to kindle the desire and smoke. Do you know what I mean?

Try to think about it: one cigarette after another, you repeated the same behaviour at certain times and places or in the presence of certain people. Maybe when you are more tired, or when you inevitably must meet that boss that you just cannot stand, etc. In short, you have associated smoking with specific situations and emotions. Could you confirm it? The context has become for you an activator of the desire that then triggers that behaviour. The cigarette completes the enjoyment of the moment. The stimulus is born, then the behaviour is activated and finally the enjoyment. The cigarette is a ritual for you. Looking at the details, we notice that there is always a message, a stimulus that triggers the mechanism of habit: words, moods, moments, other people's attitudes that can detonate the vicious circle. When the stimulus occurs, it becomes inevitable to run the entire circuit. As Charles Duhigg explains in his book *The Dictatorship of Habits*[11]:

> «First there is a signal, a switch that tells our brain to enter automatic mode and which habit to use. Then there is the routine, which can be physical, emotional or mental. Finally, there is gratification, based on which our brain decides whether it is worth memorizing a certain routine [...] Over time this circle - signal, routine, gratification - becomes more and more automatic; signal and gratification are intertwined with each other to induce a strong sense of expectation and craving, that is, need». The smoker has no control over smoking, it is an automatic behaviour. Those who think they are in control are perhaps more dependent than others who admit the opposite. In fact, if habits can be ignored, changed or replaced, it is:

---

[11] C. Duhigg, The Power of Habit: Why We Do What We Do in Life and Business, Random House Trade, 2014.

«The importance of the habit loop [...] which reveals a fundamental truth to us: when a habit is formed, the brain no longer participates in the decision-making process. He stops working or turns to other tasks. So, unless we deliberately fight against a habit - unless we find new routines - the pattern will be activated automatically».12

Smokers can constructively change their thinking, emotions and behaviours in order to break the harmful habit on which cigarette addiction is based.

Inner discomfort

The smoker can feel discomfort even when he is alone, just with himself. It also happens to non-smokers. Discomfort is a natural condition in our life. If there were no moments of discomfort, our life would be flat, we would practically do nothing new to aspire to. When I speak about discomfort, I do not mean a disease, a pathology, but a temporary feeling of lack of wellness which, in some cases, can last over time and become a more consolidated state. The discomfort can be conscious, and each of us tries to repair the loss of enthusiasm in the best possible way. The difference is that the smoker has learned to "overcome" moments of inner discomfort by smoking; on the other hand, those who do not smoke overtake them without getting intoxicated with cigarettes but doing something else. Think of smoking as a symptom, the manifestation of a tension, a stress due to an inner discomfort. Some might think: "But, at least I do not take drugs, I only smoke cigarettes". Just to be clear, as mentioned at the beginning, nicotine is a drug; furthermore, one should never compare oneself to the standards or others' results, but always measure oneself with one's own potential. It is not even useful to compare oneself to those who are worse off, in order to be able to say, "After all, I'm fine". This kind of reasoning is helpless; instead, measure yourself on the condition of wellness that you could reach and commit yourself to obtain it. The person often travels with his mind between the past and the future in situations of inner discomfort, by investing a lot of energy looking for a solution that does not exist in either of these two dimensions, because one can only act in the present. On the contrary, it is better to do it, as a friend of mine does who, in order not to think about the difficulties and release the tension, rides his bike for miles and spends his time doing physical activity. This can only make him feel better and help him find effective solutions.

Smokers believe they can use the cigarette for similar purposes; however, smoking does not make things better, but worse. In a moment of impatience,

---

12 Ivi.

fatigue, malaise (at work or at home), probably you had these kinds of thoughts too:

- "Time flies by smoking and I feel light. Otherwise the day never seems to pass ".

- "Between one cigarette and the next, I have the feeling of leaving without fatigue, and I also know that the working day is about to end".

- "Counting cigarettes has become a good way to shift attention from daily tensions. It's a countdown, and every cigarette smoked brings me closer to evening relaxation".

The smoker believes he has found the "tip" to lighten the perception of discomfort moments. Thanks to the cigarette, in fact, a temporal distortion seems to act and mitigate suffering; but the cigarette itself does nothing, it is just a smoker's conviction. However, the discomfort remains where it is, enveloped in a cloud of smoke.

The 3 beliefs

As you may have guessed, beliefs become our reality. There is no objective reality, there is a subjective one. Think of a fact or situation that is pleasant for you: it is likely that the same thing, such as a sunset, arouses happiness in you, while others evoke sadness and unpleasant memories. Everything is always seen in relation to one's own experience of events and people, based on which we attribute a meaning to it. And convictions are born from that attributed meaning. Now, we will find out what are the beliefs that grip the smoker's life, so that you are aware of them and can develop your potential. The moment you become aware of it; you will be freer!

Conviction n. 1
"There must always be something wrong in life."

Luisa grew up in a family that had to face several difficult situations. Her grandparents had experienced hard times after the war, a condition common to many families of that time. They had been able to get married with enormous efforts and sacrifices. They had lived in hardship until their grandfather got a job in a factory. Thus, they had started a more dignified life. Even if they were far from their homeland, it seemed that they had made it. They had managed to buy a house and had their first children. Everything was perfect when unfortunately the youngest son died of the flu. That world they had built with so many sacrifices collapsed. But life went on, three more children were born. Little by little Luisa's grandparents recovered, with the simplicity and joy of a loving family. It was then that another death struck the family: the eldest daughter disappeared due to leukaemia. Once again everything collapsed. Consequently, everyone in Luisa's family had a deep conviction that "things can't always go well, there must always be something wrong". In cascade, beliefs are transferred to children and beliefs generalize to everything in life. Luisa is one of those grandchildren to whom this preconception has come from afar: "You cannot be happy; life is a constant sacrifice". As if to say that in order to live it is right to always have some difficulties, in order to always suffer. That's it, it is normal. Have you noticed that when everything is going well people start saying phrases like: "It doesn't seem real to me", "Wake me up", "It is not possible" and similar thoughts? Some have the feeling that at any moment their wellness situation may be broken by some unpleasant event. It seems that at least one misfortune in life we must have to "be right" or to "guarantee" not to suffer worse tragedies, otherwise we feel different, or we have the perception of being judged by others: "Of course, for him it is easy, he has not never had any problems!" they would say.

How many do you know who think so? Or do you yourself, when you are beautifully well, have the feeling that something may be wrong? Those who think so nourish the conviction that one cannot always be happy, that "normality" is to live oppressed by difficulties. This is the mental conditioning that we undergo from an early age. For cultural, sometimes religious reasons, over the millennia they have imposed on us how to think, what is right and what is wrong. They educated us to believe that love and happiness are obtained only with sacrifice, hard work, sweat, wearing the "stigmata", as if we always had to pay the price. It is a programming, a cultural heritage that should be reinterpreted in the light of the current context and not referring to ancient scriptures. *The important thing is to be aware of these imposed patterns*. Are you familiar with the expression: "It's the only vice I have? " Do you also use it sometimes? Just to justify the cigarette. This type of smoker is difficulty oriented. If it were not the cigarette, there would be another problem. As for certain couple relationships. I choose a "cross" to carry on because life works like this. Life is one, I will never be tired of repeating it, and it must be lived at its best, erasing the pain. What do you want from your life: mediocrity, the worst or the best? The best! Then, stop lying to yourself and others. This attitude is nothing more than mental programming. When you find yourself thinking "It's the only vice I have", you will already know which mechanism is working and you will also know that you do not need vices, evils, or problems to feel good. Only actions aimed at achieving one's wellness count.

If you are good, you do not need to go looking for a difficulty. In fact, commit to getting even better and maintaining your wellness status, you know? Difficulties are moments of growth, they are preparatory to improvement; however they are only phases of life, they are not life.

Now, you have learned to recognize this pattern.

Conviction n. 2

"I am not able to succeed in life. I'm not up to par. I feel small and stupid".

The mother of all false beliefs, it is at the root of many problems that plague people today. Around this programming many people build an entire existence. They choose a partner, a job, friends and a suitable context to confirm this belief, just as they choose cigarettes.

Or rather, they adopt behaviours that support this belief. Everything confirms what they are convinced of. Luca did not know it yet, but luckily, he learned it over time. He tended to sabotage everything he did. He started a business and then abandoned it with some excuse, or he avoided it. From an early age, his parents, who wanted to protect him maybe too much, had always done everything for him, in order to make things easier for him.

They did not want him to have a hard time. They wanted the best for their son, not understanding that the best would be to leave him free to make mistakes and grow (keeping an eye on him, of course). Instead, contrary to his parents' expectations, Luca ended up developing a strong insecurity in everything he did. Insecurity generated in Luca the tendency to look for partners, jobs and friendships that confirmed his idea about himself, making him feel even more inadequate. This is an example of those beliefs: "Not being able to...". But you can do it: get rid of the cigarette, do it now if you have not already done so, because I am sure you want it. The strength is within you. Do it now! Do not listen to those who have tried to block you, to those who have prevented you from growing; even for a good purpose or in good faith, it is wrong. Protections are needed when you are small, but now you do not need them anymore, finally you are an autonomous and free person.

You can do it; you have the power to do whatever you want.

Don't agree with others. Be yourself. Choose who you want to be.

The smoker feels "small" compared to the cigarette, which he sees as a giant. Now you are starting to see it small. True, a part of you is still attracted to the cigarette, we know that well, but you are much bigger than a single part. Close your eyes and ask your unconscious: "Where are you, which part of the body is attracted to the cigarette?". Faced with this question, the answers can be very different. A person I was following pointed to my "head", because in his life there had always been someone who had decided in his place, which is why he felt confident in his ideas only when accompanied by a cigarette. Another one, on the other hand, replied "his arm" because the cigarette served as a shield in his relations with others. Surely a part of the body will come to mind to you too; as soon as this happens, be aware that it is only the one who is smoking and not everything else.

Exercise

You are no longer a smoker, only a part of you is. Isolate the part that smokes from the rest. Divide your body into areas, giving each one a specific colour. Let the free and pure part of your body shine and increase in power, more and more.

You will see that the free part will gradually overlap the part associated with the smoke; the latter will lose its intensity and then be dyed the same colour as strength and freedom. Increasingly more now!

Inhale deeply and repeat this exercise 5 times. Do it until your whole body becomes the same colour of pure energy.

Conviction n. 3

"You can always relapse!"

This belief is truly "bastard"! Such an idea seriously undermines your path to freedom. The difficulty lies in not having an objective, explicit and measurable confirmation of the new non-smoker's status. One always remains of the idea of not being free and being able to risk a relapse. All nonsense that you tell yourselves. However a, the risk becomes real because you believe it and, sooner or later, it will come true. Phil comes to me after trying to quit smoking "permanently" four times. «It's already a miracle that you wanted to come», I replied to his words. It is not easy that after several failures a smoker still wants to try; yet he was there to hope. However, it was the first time he had turned to an expert. Previously he had tried alone and with the help of nicotine substitutes.

The award for the best exhortation to quit undoubtedly went to his doctor, whose only recommendation was: "Either stop or die of cancer!". Sometimes you encounter a great communicative and relational incompetence: being so abrupt with some subjects can work, but in general it has a negative effect. Why is there the belief of a relapse? First, it is a psychological mechanism by which the ground is prepared to be able to start over, legitimizing one's insecurity as "common behaviour". In other words, a nice and good excuse. Secondly, the smoker no longer knows what life is like without a cigarette, he does not remember it. He cannot see himself without it, so he is not able to establish a standard in order to identify the transition to non-smoker. He does not know it! Finally, the context around the smoker is often not supportive, starting with the institutional figures who strongly influence the opinion of ordinary people. For example, in Italy more than 50% of doctors smoke. As well as those who hold an influential role: politicians, public and private authorities. Not to mention the parents. It is certainly not a favourable context for those who want to undertake a path of cessation!

I smoke a few ones

Smoking two or three a day is still smoking, leaving the door open to the "demon". It does not take much to go back to forty cigarettes. Precisely because at this moment you are thinking "It will never happen to me", it will almost certainly happen to you. Even if you are not thinking it now, it will still happen to you if you do not modify your thoughts, emotions and actions in order to obtain effective results for your wellness. Otherwise, when you encounter some difficulties in the future, the cigarette will always be there waiting for you and give you its "comfort". You need a new and healthy habit of life, or you will always be in check. You are a non-smoker now. I know it sounds strange, but I do not know of a clearer and more specific way to define yourself than to say what you are no longer. You are a habit of well-being. You are coming to light; a new person is born. Like a baby just out of the womb - the wonder of wonders, in my opinion - the doctor cuts the umbilical cord. From this moment, a new life begins.

I smoke the light ones

Then, there are those who say they smoke the light ones! Light? It means reading! The verb, to read? The cigarettes? Yes, then I am Napoleon! The wording *light, mild*, etc., has been eliminated for two reasons: the first is that there is nothing "light" in a cigarette whose embers reach 900° C and which releases over 4000 harmful substances for combustion; the second is psychological deception. The smoker has an altered perception of damage. Those who smoke this type of cigarettes (including *slim* ones), if they feel judged in some way for the fact of being a smoker, reply: "But they are light!". The smoker is deceived by the adjective "light", having a very low perception of the damage. But light does not mean "harmless".

Smokers of "light" cigarettes have two problems: firstly, by smoking the cigarette to the end, they inhale with more intensity; secondly, being used to a higher daily dose of nicotine, they tend not only to smoke more intensely, but also to smoke more cigarettes. Ultimately the "light" smoker either smokes more, or more intensely, or both. Result? He is more intoxicated than before. I was able to see this data on all smokers to whom in about 12 years I have checked the carbon monoxide (co). If you do not believe in what I am saying, go get a lung co check and check for yourself.

If I want to, I'll stop by myself

Getting rid of smoking is a process that starts only and exclusively from the smoker, it does not arise from the outside. It is certainly possible to free yourself from the cigarette, however it is often an excuse to continue, whether you just tell yourself or repeat it around. You certainly know many people who, despite yet another heart attack, continue to smoke undeterred. Would you call them crazy? No. Most likely you would too, even though you consider yourselves perfectly sane people. "If I want to just quit" is just one of the excuses that smokers tell themselves not to admit, always for that spirit of self-preservation inherent in man, that he is doing something against himself. On the other hand, he also feels the need to show others that he is in control of the situation. I have seen this kind of twisted reasoning in thousands of smokers. The addiction to cigarettes is so strong that it causes smokers to deny the real risks to their health, both to themselves and to their loved ones. I gave the example of a heart attack, but I could make a similar argument by citing pulmonary emphysema, circulatory problems and other even more serious diseases, such as the devastating "Buerger's disease", also known as obliterating trombangioitis. This tragic disease is strongly linked to cigarette smoking and manifests itself with poor circulation in small and medium-sized arteries and veins, with particular attention to the limbs. It can also manifest itself with the reduction of tactile and thermal sensitivity, up to the amputation of the lower limbs if the consumption of cigarettes is not immediately stopped and specific care is taken.

The professor Phil Brancato, friend and teacher on smoking, said, during an awareness tour that we conducted in 2005 in forty institutes in Massachusetts, of his direct acquaintance, a firefighter, heavy smoker:

«I knew a firefighter who after retirement and despite his health problems continued undaunted to smoke. He at first, he started to have tingling legs and poor circulation, however he continued to smoke. Difficulty walking later. He continued to smoke. Then, his leg was amputated. He continued. The other one. Finally, he died of a heart attack».

I sincerely thank prof. Brancato for all the things he taught me, and this book also wants to be the testimony of a generous person who, without asking for anything in return went far and wide in order to persuade smokers to change their lives and educate the youngest. He has not been with us for a few years, but I would have liked to have given him this book. I just need to know how many will finally be free from the cigarette. Now, let's get back to us: if you recognize yourself in one of the excuses, I mentioned but do not know how to react to it, do not be discouraged! Start by taking note. Whatever you notice as part of your character sphere, your habits and attitudes, you can first identify it and then modify it in such a way that it is productive and useful for your well-being.

Women, children and smoking

Unfortunately, all the beauty of a woman goes up in smoke with the cigarette. I will be against the trend; it is my opinion. The curious aspect of the matter is that, as far as I have noticed, smokers are the first to recognize that smoking bothers and makes us ugly. Women especially compared to men. Being generally more attentive to aesthetics, it is the smokers themselves who admit that smoking damages women's beauty and health. So, once again the statement "If I want to, I'll stop by myself" is not true. The topic is particularly close to my heart because when it comes to women, motherhood is somehow involved. Many women who claim to be able to quit smoking on their own believe they can do so during pregnancy. One in three pregnant women continues to smoke13. Women who continue to smoke during pregnancy can seriously harm the foetus and the health of the unborn child. Do you think they are unworthy mothers? Crazy? Irresponsible?

I think they love the creature in their womb like all other mothers, however the addiction to cigarettes is so powerful that it pushes them to create absurd excuses and justifications in order to continue. On the other hand, I believe that paediatricians and doctors who recommend smoking up to 5 cigarettes a day are

---

13 Moige - Movimento Italiano Genitori Onlus, "I danni del fumo in gravidanza: alcuni dati", http://www.moige.it/news-i-danni-del-fumo-in-gravidanza-alcuni-dati-611269#

condemned. From my point of view, they are just missing professionals, unable to provide the right strategies to help the expectant mother quit smoking. Many women repeat: "I quit when I want", "I quit when I am pregnant", are lulled into addiction because they have heard from other women that they quit during pregnancy. In fact, in some cases it is possible that the decrease or cessation of smoking occurs naturally in the nine months before giving birth. Sometimes future mothers feel repulsion and nausea towards the cigarette because in pregnancy endogenous substances are released that create a new balance in the woman for which the stimulation of nicotine is not necessary. However, the phenomenon is not the rule, but the exception. It will therefore be useful to clarify what the consequences of smoking during pregnancy may be, even if perhaps for someone it will already be known:

- underweight unborn child.

- damage to the nervous system of the new born, with the manifestation of long-lasting neuro-behavioural discomfort.

- predisposition to respiratory diseases such as asthma.

- SDS ("sudden death syndrome"), or rather the cot death of the infant. This is an unexplained and sudden death, which appears to be strongly related to smoking.

- death of the foetus in the womb.

As you can guess, these are risks that are best known to avoid, not cure. Yet, even if this information is in the public domain, there are mothers who continue to smoke during pregnancy and fathers who smoke in the presence of their pregnant wife or partner. So, if you are a smoking father, first remember to smoke away from the place where your wife or partner is. You can also advise, inform and help your female to make the decision to eliminate smoking during gestation. It should be added, however, that the negative action on children can also occur after birth: if you smoke in the same environments as your home, car, office, children become helpless victims of parental addiction, which can cause damage irreversible to their health. In addition to the above considerations on women, I must inform men that smoking can drastically reduce the production of spermatozoa and affect their motility, or the ability they must move. The risk is sterility or difficulty in fertilizing the woman's egg. I wanted to insert "strong" information not to impress and frighten you, but only to sensitize, inform and educate you. If you want to continue smoking, go ahead, but safeguard those who cannot rebel. But stop saying "If I want to just stop": smoking is an addiction. And if you are here you know it and are looking for help. Stop saying, "I'll do it when I'm pregnant", because you might be one of the many moms who keep smoking.

There is time

Another curious smoker's aspect is that he absolutely does not have the problem of quitting up to the age of thirty, he does not think about it at all. If you ask him, he replies: "Stop?!? And why? I like smoking!"

Going on with age and up to about sixty, he answers the same question: "Yes, in fact I am thinking of quitting because I often cough and then I do not have the same physique as when I was twenty, now can feel my breathlessness. I am decreasing slowly. Now, I stop. As soon as the holidays arrive, I stop… ". These are often the "famous last words". Thoughts of this kind only postpone the decision. Now retired, the smoker thinks differently and to the same question, "Quit smoking?". He replies: "Now at my age it is no longer of any use. By now the damage has been done, it can no longer be recovered. We might as well continue; the important thing is young people. I always tell my children and my grandchildren not to be like me!" What an incredible reasoning! One would think that smoking affects the brain much harder than it is said! Do you realize that the pensioner in question is the same person who forty years earlier said he did not want to quit because he liked him? There always seems to be a good reason to continue smoking and postpone the decision: "There is time to quit!"

Training

When military training is carried out, those that save the skin in war, exactly the conditions that will be encountered in the most difficult moment are showed up. For you, the training will be here with me and out there in everyday life you will live your most difficult times. Maybe you will enjoy putting these tips and conditioning into practice in your everyday life. Maybe you will take the risk and end up having a laugh, and in what you thought was a difficult situation you will say: "But look, he was right". Do not laugh now!

If you think "This is not the right time", it means that it is the right time! The simulation must be realistic to be effective and save your skin! Think of a drug addict. Not of you, another one. Let's tell someone who uses drugs, not nicotine, another one. Drug users do it a few times a week or, in the worst cases, a few times a day. A smoker smokes 20-30 cigarettes a day. Are you aware that the smoker repeats the gesture and reinforcement 20 times or more a day?

It should be added that smoking is socializing, while other drugs marginalize. For this reason, there is an altered perception of the phenomenon, which is why it should not be underestimated. Some of the bad excuses that many smokers repeat are: "I have no addiction, at least this one!", "I don't do drugs, I don't do things outside the box, etc.". In short, nonsense of this kind. Do you find yourself? Have you ever had any similar thoughts? I really think so. Well, do you know why? Due to the "must"! Yes, the "must" you have in your head! As children we were programmed to the sound of: "This is done", "This is right", "This is not done", "It must be done as I say", etc. Did it happen to you too, or just me?

Therefore the smoker's tendency is to say: "It's the only vice!"... The only vice compared to what? Where is the list of virtues and vices that we must or can have? What are the parameters? The parameters are those imposed by others. Saying "It's the only vice" means that I normally follow the rules as a good child, but every now and then I give myself an extra, which in turn means "I want to do what I want". Are you there? Is that clear to you now?

Mass persuasion

It is essential to understand how and why you have this high regard for the cigarette, this fatal attraction.

If someone knew what you are like, what are the psychological levers to activate to get inside your mind, your weaknesses and strengths, they would almost certainly succeed. Marketers and advertisers know this very well. I can assure you that advertisers know their children's needs far more than parents. This is what happened with the cigarette: you think you chose it, when it was all planned thanks to media conditioning, which created a habit widespread and social behaviour to emulate. So, you defend it.

Your opinion of the cigarette has been artfully packaged, as the journalism and communication expert Marcello Foa explains very well. It was a creation at the table of the communicating professionals, indeed of the manipulation, to have made the cigarette become a symbol of social rebellion and transgression for our culture. First, by creating the myth of an emancipated and sexually free woman thanks to the cigarette. The "woman" who smokes, in fact, is not sensual in the act she makes, but it is the result of an emotional connection created primarily by advertising and then disseminated by films. Some might think that the *cigarette-emancipation* association is due to the directors of the 1950s, who introduced the cigarette on the set.

Instead it dates to an even earlier era. It was not a spontaneous process, but a link artfully implanted by the father of the *spin doctors*, Edward L. Bernays.

The spin doctor is defined by the Oxford Dictionary as "a spokesperson hired to give a favourable interpretation of events to the media, especially on behalf of a political party"14. In simpler terms, the *spin doctor* manipulates the information to be delivered to the media for the benefit of an institution, party, company in order to influence the masses. Specifically, in 1929 Bernays was hired by a large tobacco company to increase sales. The expert devised a truly powerful strategy of persuasion and mass manipulation. Marcello Foa explains:

> «On Easter day [...] at the torchlight procession of the liberty brigade he enrolled and paraded some beautiful models, dressed in a very provocative way for the time, or rather, with pants, blouse, suspenders, a beret on the head reclined. Beautiful, haughty, charming, and he showed them off, smoking ostentatiously. Also look at the meaning of the words: the brigade has a positive value, freedom in American society is a positive value, the torchlight procession evokes the cigarette. Result: endless controversies, raging articles in the press, "it is the decay of the times", "where will we end up?", And so on. Immediate result: the sales of cigarettes quadrupled and this idea of rebellion associated with smoking that has entered the collective consciousness».15

The *cigarette-emancipation* association that thus became implanted in the collective consciousness is so powerful that it still affects the smoker today, strengthened by the ad campaigns of the tobacco farms that over time have entered the groove traced by Bernays, generating myths that have remained etched in the collective imagination. Remember those old Marlboro commercials that featured cowboys? Physically attractive, virile, invincible, they have contributed to creating a powerful association between the idea of smoking and the representation of male strength, by generating the myth of the smoking man "who must never ask", an emblematic image of masculinity. But you may not know the consequences of smoking on the protagonists of the myth. In fact, the

---

14 Ibidem.

15 Ibidem.

Marlboro men[16], the commercial cowboys died because of the cigarette: two of them (Wayne McLaren and David McLean) were struck by lung cancer; David Millar Jr. died of pulmonary emphysema. Shortly before he died, McLaren had become an anti-tobacco advocate.

You are not a man only if you smoke, you are a man regardless! There are other canons that indicate being a man, father, leader and example for others, certainly not the cigarette. A person addicted to a drug, a toxic substance cannot be taken as an example, he can never become a leader. One last example to conclude this topic: you may have seen one of those movies or advertisements in which, after a night of sex, the two lovers smoke a cigarette: this is also a "sex = cigarette" connection. A powerful emotional anchor is created through images, which unconsciously conditions the behaviour of consumers by leveraging their needs and desires. Advertisers know exactly what happens, and how to get it. Anything you attribute to the cigarette in terms of positive value is false; they made fun of you, they manipulated you just to sell you a product. Once inside, addiction takes care of it. Now you know and you can begin to choose *free-of-mind*.

Other aids

Use all that can be useful to you smartly. I mean all the initiatives that empower you as an individual, that stimulate your commitment, awareness and personal power.

At the same time, as the path suggested in this book, you can also:

- participate in group or individual sessions at the Anti-Smoking Centres in the area.
- practice autogenic training.
- do meditation.
- use nicotine substitutes (if necessary and under medical supervision).
- use the vaporizer (electronic cigarette) for a limited period.

---

16 E. Di Pasqua, "Addio a Eric Lawson, quinto Marlboro Man ucciso dalla sigaretta", «Corriere della Sera» 24/01/2014; http://www.corriere.it/salute/sportello_cancro/14_gennaio_27/addio-eric-lawson-marlboro-man-ucciso-sigaretta-0149e70c-8746-11e3-b7c5-5c15c6838f80.shtml

- do acupuncture or electrostimulation.

- read other books that you think will help you.

In short, do whatever you think will help you, except move on to other addictions: people and/or substances. As for the use of drugs, in cases of extreme necessity, if taken as a support - and not as a substitute - to their commitment within the framework of a specific path, they can concretely assist in smoking cessation, as demonstrated by the Guidelines of the Higher Institute for health. I would like to clarify this because we live in an era in which we are very easily seeking the solution to our problems in drugs, rather than realizing the importance of so-called primary prevention and therefore of adopting a healthy lifestyle. And this is precisely what I want to aim for with you: I believe in our personal power to improve ourselves and achieve wellness. I continually push people to bring out their potential. In order to do this, you must take full responsibility for your own growth. You cannot continue to delegate others, or anything else!

Lose weight without cigarettes

I'm not crazy! You got it right, by quitting smoking you will be able to lose weight. In fact, I'll tell you more: maybe it will be even easier for you than when you smoked. As soon as I say something like this, my clients often reply: "But I've already been there!", "My father gained 20 kg after quitting!", "What are you saying?! It is well known that you gain weight!", etc. This is also a form of defence. The conditioned mind always plays the same role: protecting you from a change by triggering a thousand doubts and resistances.

The smoker's mental process works like this:

1. You want to quit smoking because you feel a sense of guilt within you: on the one hand, you know that it hurts you and that you are throwing away your money; on the other hand, you also know that it bothers your loved ones, your children, partner and friends, who perhaps have also told you outright and repeatedly tell you to stop. In short, there is a desire to quit, even if with a thousand hesitations.

2. You take action to get a result, then you take the package and throw it away. If you are among those who think they must prove they are strong, I would say "badass", leave the package in plain sight by promising not to be tempted. Have you ever wondered why the smoker, in general, wants to quit smoking while keeping the pack of cigarettes on the piece of furniture at home?

   For the same reason he started: in order to give the idea of being strong. You say to yourself: "I quit, and I have to be stronger than him (referring to that damn pack of cigarettes)! I put it here in front of my eyes, like my father did when he quit. He put it on the bedside table and never touched a cigarette!"

   What does this mean? Which always commands the same pattern, by virtue of which the subject in question is always there, trying to hide his fragility. By doing so, it is likely that in one way or another he will always remain a smoker, because he will not be able to break with his old identity deep down. It is like leaving the photo of an ex on the bedside table. If you are no longer together, the photo must be removed, you do not care anymore. It is a broken relationship.

3. Then start telling the closest people that you are "trying" to quit. You are careful not to give a certainty, in fact you are not convinced. When you are alone you repeat to yourself: "No, man, I must do it!", "It is not possible that a cigarette will win and not me!" Admit it: do not you do this bullshit too?

4. Get started. First day: "I feel good, I don't miss it at all"; the second day: "I'm fine, I miss a little gesture"; from the third day: "I'm getting hungrier, but I'm not smoking. I eat a little more, but I don't smoke!" True?

Here is the best part! Because what you want is to stop, and so far, we agree. You would also like to be in good physical shape, or at least not get fat, and we agree on this too, right? *(If by chance you are one of those people who call themselves lazy, who doesn't care if they weigh 100 kg or more because they are fine, who could give up everything except for eating, well, I continue to respect you as a person even though I don't share this harmful lifestyle. Because, if this is the case, it is you who do not respect each other, the same as you do with smoking).*

However, if you are convinced that quitting smoking automatically makes you fat, as if you have a sword of Damocles on your head, you will experience a great conflict between two important goals. Do you agree? The first is to quit smoking, which I would better translate as "being smoke-free"; the second is to have a satisfactory physical shape, or at least keep the current one. However, if by reaching the first you lose the second, that would be a big problem. So, you think you are forced to give up one of the two goals. Which one to choose? Continue to smoke and maintain your weight or quit and gain weight? Bad business! Could your self-esteem ever allow you to gain weight? Of course not! It means that it will go to great lengths to sabotage your intent to quit. How? Pushing you to devour junk, to increase portions, to eat after hours.

Do you know why you would do it? Just to get to the limit allowed by your scales and to hear yourself say from your inner voice: "You cannot continue to gain weight like this, start smoking again! You were better off when you smoked! ". Smoking is a manifestation of low self-esteem, but you and I know it, not the others who meet you on the street. Being out of shape or terribly fat, on the other hand, is an obvious discomfort even in the others' eyes and therefore affects you more. The aesthetic factor facilitates relationships. The more fit and attractive you feel, the easier it is to relate, especially with the opposite sex. People will then choose smoking between smoking and fat. Smoking always has its charm, much less fat. Did you understand that all these stories you tell in your head are just bullshit? Which are triggered as a protection mechanism to prevent change?

When you are immersed in a process of changing to a desired state (*being free from the cigarette*) you feel a certain degree of discomfort. Food allows abstinence to be somewhat attenuated because it produces a sensation of pleasure by stimulating the production of a neurotransmitter, dopamine, also known as the "happiness' hormone". Unconsciously, food is used as a scapegoat: however, by eating to excess, you end up damaging your health, undermining your physical shape and your image, and consequently the opinion you have of yourself and that which others have about you, and returning to smoking becomes the solution to the new problem. All of this is a creation of your mind, it is not real. It is just a mechanism that your mind creates to sabotage the detachment from smoking and push you to take the cigarette back, with the excuse that basically you were better off before. Now that you know this, you will learn to recognize when this mechanism is in action.

Abstinence

«Everyone agrees that cigarette smoking is one of the biggest addiction generators. The chemical hooks of tobacco derive from a drug contained in it, called nicotine. When nicotine patches were invented in the early 1990s, there was a great deal of optimism - smokers could enjoy all the beloved chemical hooks without the dirty (and deadly) contraindications of smoking. They would have been "free".

But the Directorate-General for Health found that just 17.7 percent of cigarette smokers can quit using nicotine patches. Now, that is not cheap. If chemicals account for 17.7 % of addiction, as has been shown, we are still talking about millions of lives being ruined around the world. But what we discover, once again, is that the story we have been taught about chemical hooks as the Cause of Addiction, although true, is only a fragment within a larger mosaic»*17*..

According to the studies of Dr. Benowits, *the withdrawal caused by nicotine* is the same as that created by *cocaine*.18Only towards the third day after cessation do the first withdrawal symptoms begin, which can last up to about fifteen days later. What does abstinence consist of? Physical discomfort: sweating, stomach cramps, finger shaking, difficulty concentrating, etc. Not always all these symptoms appear, sometimes just some of them; they can also vary in intensity depending on the person and the situation in which they find themselves. I'll explain in a simple way the mechanism of smoking addiction:

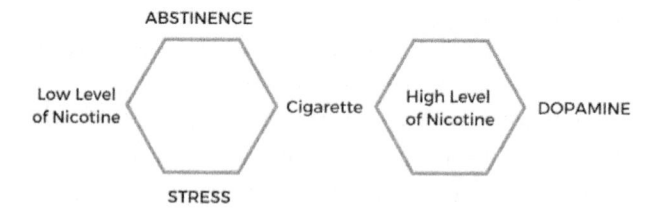

```
         ABSTINENCE
            ⬡
Low Level       High Level
of Nicotine  Cigarette  of Nicotine   DOPAMINE
            ⬡
          STRESS
```

As already mentioned, the human body naturally produces, a neurotransmitter, *dopamine*, the famous "happiness' hormone", whenever we satisfy a pleasure. However, nicotine in turn prevents the *natural production* of dopamine in the smoker and this causes restlessness. Therefore, nicotine first inhibits dopamine

---

17 J. Hari, op. cit.

18 M. De Biasi, "Meccanismi biologici della dipendenza da nicotina", «Tabaccologia», 2006, 1S, 19-23; http://www.tabaccologia.it/PDF/1S_2006/5_1S_2006.pdf

and then controls its release. We can say that the cigarette controls the production and inhibition of dopamine. What happens after a period without smoking? Imagine that you have a container inside of you in which nicotine collects when you smoke. After a period of abstinence, this container begins to empty. Nicotine gradually leaves the body through the urine. It is no coincidence that it is suggested to drink a lot of water to accelerate the body's purification process, as soon as it has stopped. As nicotine drops, we enter the phase of abstinence and stress which becomes a stimulus to light the next cigarette. Smoking restores the nicotine level by filling the "dedicated" container and the dopamine's secretion is stimulated, giving that feeling of "pleasure" and satisfaction that lasts until the level is lowered again and so on forever. Is there no limit? Smoking indefinitely warns of abuse. The diehard smokers, who must smoke even before falling asleep, know this feeling quite well.

So, returning to the mechanism of physical addiction, we can summarize by saying that without dopamine you suffer, and when it is produced you are better. It is now clear to you that it is not nicotine that generates the pleasant sensation, but dopamine. Due to nicotine, the natural dopamine release system is altered, it works abnormally. The smoker, on the other hand, is convinced that it is the cigarette that makes him feel good and connects a sense of "pleasure" to it, he attributes a positive value to it as if he inhaled dopamine directly from the cigarette. It is wrong, I'm sorry to disappoint the "still smokers".

Exercise

Since it is the cigarette the cause of discomfort, from now on, when you think about the cigarette, I want you to associate it with the moments of suffering and abstinence. Dwell intensely on these thoughts and press the index finger and thumb of the left-hand Fig. 4 (PISX) together. So, when you experience withdrawal symptoms, you smile and think: "You don't fool me anymore, you are the cause of this malaise! If I smoke, you I'll continue to feel so bad... fuck you!". Don't laugh, I'm serious. You think this is just a transition phase and that soon you will be even better than before.

«After the first phase of the "mouse park", Professor Alexander carried out the test. He went back to repeating the original experiments, those in which the mice were left alone and compulsively used drugs. He let them use it for fifty-seven days - an amount of time enough to hook them up. Then, he took them out of isolation, placing them inside the "mouse park". He wanted to understand if, once an addiction developed, the brain was so altered that it could no longer recover. If drugs took over you. What happened was - once again - amazing. The mice showed some withdrawal problems, but soon stopped using them intensively, returning to live a normal life. The good cage had saved them.»19

Now press the thumb and index finger of the left hand (PISX) between them, read on and keep your grip. How do you feel at the end of a massage? Experience a pleasant sensation, experience wellness. This is pleasure! And if you have been carrying a weight of 100 kg on your back for years and replace it with a 50 kg weight for a day, what would you feel like? Would you like it? Of course yes. The same pleasure as a massage? No, because it is not real pleasure, it is only a lessening of pain. Healthy and real pleasure is that experienced by addition, not by subtraction. I will explain clearly. If you suffer and something relieves the pain you are not experiencing pleasure, but less pain. If anything you can call it relief. Pleasure is what you feel when making love, or when you laugh out loud; or after a massage, or when you dedicate yourself to doing the things you love the most: a sport, a hobby, etc. Pleasure is pleasure, no less pain, not mere relief. You are aware that you still have 50 kg on your back, right? Another 50 kg weighs on your health.

Trust or hope

Many people believe that the solution, wellness, happiness come on their own, with the help of a little luck sooner or later. I think they come as a result of our decisions. As Tony Robbins puts it, decisions are shaping our future. In all fields. *Hoping* can be catastrophic sometimes. It is a mental attitude that indicates helplessness. Delegating to others, to something else, one's success is not ideal and for the realization of a goal. Having confidence in oneself and in one's own possibilities, on the other hand, is an indispensable element for the realization of a goal; at the same time, it involves taking responsibility, leaving no room for excuses and justifications. This is the ideal mental attitude to start "deciding". And making a decision is everything. By hoping "decisions" are not made, we let ourselves go. In trust, on the other hand, the best decisions are made, those that, regardless of the consequences and results, make them available for learning, to welcome what arrives, without excuses or recriminations. The ability to make decisions is essential for everyone's life. The difficulty of many lies precisely in being used to undergoing life, without acting in decisions: people, the others' choices, situations undergo. The smoker suffers from the "Prophet" syndrome. He already knows how he will end up, so he does not decide, he leaves himself to

---

19 J. Hari, op. cit.

destiny which, by definition, is already written regardless. The smoker tends to be fatalistic and considers events as warning signs, in a way that is distorted by his own vision. But those who are convinced that they have no control over their life, whatever they do can never change things. Whatever happens will never get better if it is not written in destiny. If you have a fatalistic attitude towards life, you risk living in perennial frustration, the daughter of passive acceptance, contenting yourself. In this way of seeing things, there is neither activation nor commitment, and even less, a captivating vision of the future.

How different is life when you decide!

→ There is a proactive attitude.

→ an empowering vision of the future.

→ gratitude for the present.

→ confidence in the possibility.

→ to change things and succeed.

→ awareness of control.

→ a lot of energy despite everything.

Don't underestimate the power of your decisions!

How to notice the change

Many people reply: "By quitting smoking!". No, you are out of the way!

Behaviour is the last step, the tip of the iceberg. Change has very deep roots and can manifest itself in various ways. You will feel the change - maybe you already feel it now - because you had or will have an enlightenment, new thoughts and ideas that will open your mind, hearing your inner voice suggesting things you have never said before and you will open your eyes, saying: "Oops! It's happening! Change! Here we are!" or you will simply experience new sensations. Maybe you will continue to smoke in the meantime, but as I told you the change is not necessarily seen in that. It is possible that you feel unpleasant, uncomfortable sensations, but do not worry they are often signing of activation of change.

You may feel your back tense or relax than usual, rapid heartbeat, or a change in your breathing. I remember a boy named Marc who one day ran into my office saying: "I'm sick, my heart has gone mad, what should I do? What's happening to me?" Marc had the classic symptoms of nicotine abstinence: tachycardia and tremor. Being a particularly anxious type certainly did not help him: having interrupted the reassuring ritual of the cigarette, he felt lost. "These sensations are normal at first" I assured him, "try to breathe regularly, relax your body".

Exercise

Now you too relax with me: start taking a deep breath, and while you do it open and welcome the change within you, just for you, feeling the energy of *your wellness*, pervading you; every cell in your body feeds and acquires the colour you like best.

Everything is coloured and your energy becomes more and more, and you feel that it passes through and fills every single part of your body: your feet, legs, pelvis, belly and then again, your back, neck, head as in a relaxing massage, and as it passes, it purifies any resistant thought, until it descends into the throat.

Keep it up, inside your belly the energy floods your organs, your heart, what a beautiful colour! Everything is coloured with your favourite colour, keep going, you are doing well. Change means improvement for you.

Change = Improvement

Repeat with me:

• I can change!

• I want to do it!

• Now I can change!

• I want to do it now!

• I feel full of energy and I want to live 100%!

(I did not hear! Out loud and hand on heart, repeat 3 times with me!)

This is not an exercise to convince oneself, but a training in self-awareness. I show you its effectiveness. Follow me.

> Repeat aloud, hand on heart, very slowly, in a calm, deep and firm voice:
>
> 1. I... can... change!
>
> 2. I ... want to ... do it!
>
> 3. Now... I... can... change!
>
> 4. I ... I want to... do it... now!
>
> 5. I feel full of energy... and... I want to live 100%!

Do it repeatedly. Very good. Do it again before continuing.

How do you feel? From now on, repeat the exercise every day.

Time distortion

The question of time affects everyone, smokers and non-smokers. There is a lot of talk about "time management", but do you know how to manage your time? Does your time support you or follow you? Does it make you feel good, or does it generate heaviness? How many times have you experienced moments that seemed like an eternity? Remember the first kiss as teenagers in love? Did it seem to you too that it lasted an eternity? Did not the last holidays you have taken have flown away in a moment? Remember math time? Did it seem to you that it would never end?

Is it true or not that when you smoke it seems that time passes quickly, thus lightening the day and, when you are stuck in a nerve-wracking wait, one cigarette leads to another? Finally, it's time to sleep, with the last cigarette and the bed waiting for you. As you may have understood, I am not talking about clock time, but how we perceive it. When we are in a condition that generates discomfort, we use tricks with which we can somehow change the perception of time and space. Or rather, we can move our minds to other places, in order to expand or reduce the perceived time to our advantage.

What happens while smoking? Why if a smoker does not smoke, the hours and minutes go by so slowly? The answer is in the bond it has created with time. The smoker implements a time distortion every time he smokes. Let me explain in certain situations, the smoker develops the habit of taking a cigarette, lighting it and starting to smoke.

He does it to release tension, to try to dissolve an inner malaise. Over time, with the consolidation of the habit, it ends up unknowingly creating a stimulus-response association so that when you smoke a cigarette it automatically implements a temporal distortion, easing the tensions of the moment.

It is no coincidence that the best times to smoke are work breaks, minutes in which we disconnect from the routine of every day, fragments of the everyday cut out for themselves, you know what I mean. In other words, by smoking, the smoker has the impression that the day goes by more quickly and therefore is less subjected to the suffering that certain circumstances or life situations cause him. Smoking becomes a form of time control. As the runner gives himself a rhythm by keeping an inner count, so the life of the smoker is marked by cigarettes. As if cigarettes gave a measure of one's path and its progress. The inner count allows the runner to abstract from the clock time and create a personal one, much more suited to himself. The ride becomes shorter, as well as the path, everything is much less tiring. Thus, the day for the smoker. But it is important to note that it is only a mental construction and, since you manage it, you can do the same for your own wellness. Now, allow yourself to be free to live every moment of your life from a well-being perspective. Leave your mind light, breathe deeply, feel better disposed. When you were a child you did it very well, then someone told you to keep your feet on the ground. Your mind needs to dream, help it do it at all times of the day and enjoy the well-being that always comes with it. It is not the cigarette that relaxes you, before it did it because it was just a link. Relaxation is the fruit of your mind and you can train and reproduce it at any time of the day. Later, I will teach you how to use the time distortion strategy as you please.

Accept the situation and yourself

Smokers, as addicted to nicotine, are nothing more than nicotine addicts. Do not you agree with me? Being called a "nicotine addict" bothers me, I know, but it is the reality. It is who you are, at least if you smoke. Moreover, "cocaine addict" and "heroin addict" are the terms used to define the users of their respective drugs. Now, I test you. Are you ready? From smokers, you now go on to be nicotine addicts. Being a nicotine addict means being addicted to nicotine, right? Nicotine is a toxic substance, isn't it? Did you know that by taking the amount of nicotine contained in thirty cigarettes in a single dose, an adult would die from poisoning? Let us return to the most important issue, your identity. If you are addicted to nicotine, which is a toxic substance, then you are an *addict*! It can be difficult for you to accept this. I get it. If you do not feel like it, stop here. But, if you want to make a difference and put an end to the cigarette, continue, accept to wear these clothes, because they are the ones that belong to you, at least for now. I warned you from the beginning that it would be a demanding job. I am not interested in being likeable to you, my aim is for you to reach the goal. If you are curious about what might happen, read Tiffany's story. I tell you about her because she is the most emblematic case of resistance and transformation that I have been able to witness. Tiffany showed up in my office as a purposeful, strong woman who knows what she wants from life. In short, she is one of those tough and determined. Yet she needed to be a little more self-aware and understand why she smoked. In fact, admitting that you are a smoker is not enough to be aware and wake up. She takes a lot more. Precisely for this reason she was very resistant to doing the exercise you are about to do. One afternoon, during one of the interviews, I said to her: "Tiffany, repeat with me: I'm a drug addict!" Total silence. A block. First pale, then red and angry. She jumped up and walked away. Other times it had happened that someone stiffened, but after the initial hesitation they had always followed me. Instead, this time Tiffany had a fit of anger, a revulsion. She was offended.

Exercise

Repeat with me:

"I am a drug addict! "

Repeat 3 times aloud and keep pressed the index and thumb of the left hand (PISX). You must empathize, identify with what you are repeating, until you really feel that way.

How does the idea of being a drug addict make you feel?

I know I am a drug addict and I am scared. I don't want to be

Imagine you see a drug addict on the street. What sensations does it give you, what do you think of him? Write your considerations down here:

I feel sorry for them. I wonder what

has made them so addicted.

What you have just described is *your opinion about yourself*!

You now have a point of reference from which to start changing your mind. Put yourself in this person's shoes and feel like him; try to see yourself as he sees himself. How do you perceive yourself in this state? How do others see you? What is their opinion about you? What do they say about you?

I feel sad, scared, trapped. I feel other's looking at me with pity. I think they are disgusted by me, try to avoid me. Feel like I have hit rock bottom.

While rereading, hold down (PISX) the index and thumb of the left hand. Within minutes you were promoted once again. You are now on a higher level, the highest! Congratulations... you are addicted!

Repeat 3 times, aloud, keeping the thumb and index finger of the left hand pressed together (PISX):
I am a drug addict!
I am a drug addict!
I am a drug addict!

From now on, when you think about cigarettes, or have the urge to smoke one, at the idea of being drug addicts, when you see yourself as you are, you will have to squeeze the index finger and thumb of your left hand (PISX) together. Your left hand is connected to the cigarette and everything that comes with it. Forefinger and thumb pressed together. Understood? Join the fingers of the left hand as if to do ok! You don't have to quit smoking now; it will happen soon. If you quit, resume (no, I'm kidding!). Read this paragraph again, repeat all the exercises, focus your attention on your new identity, strengthen it. Do this until you have accepted your identity as a drug addict.

If you think you are already aware of your addiction, and therefore need not dwell on it, you are making a mistake. If you are in a hurry to move on to quit earlier, you can do it, however I suggest you wait, you do not have to break free now. As soon as you feel it, I repeat, you *will feel* inside you - you will not "think" but feel - that you are fully aware of your real status, you can keep going on. Of course it is not an easy job! The "magic" needs commitment, discipline and mistakes to be able to accomplish. And if in the meantime you want to find out what happened to Tiffany, read below.

Tiffany called me a few days after that instinctive flight. She apologized for her behaviour. I thought she would not feel like continuing. I was wrong. Instead, a very interesting thing happened. Her rejection of the sentence "I am a drug addict" was so strong that it prompted her to repeat herself repeatedly:

> «I will never say that I am a drug addict», «I will never repeat "I am a drug addict"». For a few days, Tiffany repeated this litany in her head. She repeated it so many times that she made it her own, that she identified with it. In short, she became the best at practicing this exercise. She returned transformed. She was another person. She was convinced and felt like a drug addict. This paved the way for her to continue with the meetings and quit smoking, but she would never have succeeded if she had not completed the exercise. If it helps, then use Tiffany's strategy: "I'll never repeat... I'm a drug addict!"

6 MOTIVATION

«The bigger the why,

the easier the how».

Jim Rohn

When Rihanna, 35, came for a consultation, I remember she said to me, «I've tried them all, I'm coming to you out of conscience. I already know that you will not stop! ».

Me: «But you don't have to stop, you are still young...!».

R.: «But, what are you saying?! I want to stop; I can't take it anymore! ».

Me: «Convince me. You give me good reasons why I should help you! ».

She said to me with playful eyes: "It has become a prison and I want to get out of."

So, I promised Rihanna that I would help her, on the condition that she was committed to doing whatever I asked her to do. In order to begin, I gave her a form to fill out: writing her would help to clarify her personal motivation. She was torn too, just like you. Her cigarette seemed to be stronger. And you? Are you willing to follow my advice? To change? What goals, what prospects do you have? In this chapter we will explore several aspects and potentials related to these questions.

Let's start with an exercise that helps us explore our motivations.

Exercise

Now imagine that you are twenty years older and find yourself in a situation you would never want to find yourself in: a serious illness due to cigarettes.

> Think hard about the situation, focus the colours, sharpen the details, magnify them. You are inside the scene, amplify the voices, the sensations and press the index finger and thumb of the left hand together (PISX). Left hand!
>
> Do this 5 times. Imagine the scene, step it up, PISX.
>
> From now and, for the next 30 days, repeat the exercise 1-2 times a day, with attention and commitment. You and only you, can make a difference. I will stand by you, together we will succeed!

The life I don't want

The smoker often has not been "seen" by someone who considered important to him or feels that he has been treated as invisible; and perhaps even today, although he is now an adult, this "someone" does not "see", notice, pay the attention he thinks he deserves, or it is the smoker himself who continues to nurture this belief. As a result, many smokers tend to have low self-esteem. This dynamic is triggered in the relationship with the significant figures, which usually are the parents. In these cases, "not to be seen" also means not having received the support necessary to follow one's inclinations. It is not easy to accept not being seen, I know. Ask yourself, "What if so? What and how would *my* point of view on smoking change?". This question can bring back memories and unpleasant situations, but also decisive answers. This is the case of Lucia, one of the people who struck me the most among the many I encountered. When I met her, I was impressed: Lucia was radiantly beautiful. Her cigarette had nothing to do with her, so bright, elegant, fine. Too obvious dystonia. I thought she had come to ask for information for her husband or a loved one, but she admitted, she was the one who smoked a pack a day. Her beauty, when it is objective, jumps in the eyes: one cannot fail to notice it and not perceive it out of tune notes. "What's behind this woman's smoke? What supports and pushes the cigarette? What is the discomfort she hides? What does the cigarette help you?" I asked myself, and then the person directly concerned. After the initial hesitation, and the complex compilation of answers, Lucia told me that these questions had been a fundamental input for her, because they had helped her realise: «I finally understood why I smoke. It took me a lot of years but that's enough now, I want to quit for good!».

Lucia understood that her addiction to her stemmed from the feeling of not being seen for what she had inside her. As if that label of "beautiful" that she had been given to her from an early age did not allow her to express her qualities. At the same time, the cigarette was the clumsy means with which Lucia tried to communicate to the world the need to be seen for what she had inside her and not just for her own appearance. Smoking had been for her a way to attract the attention of her parents and growing up to be accepted by others regardless of her beauty. For twenty years, she had remained tied to this false belief. When she realized this, I said to her, «Take your last cigarette, write 'I am not seen' on it and smoke it. And immediately after that, throw away any supplies you have. Destroy them, throw them away in the bin. Don't give them away, don't keep them. It is not a sin to throw them away. You are also protecting those around you. You don't bring unnecessary problems; you don't have to justify what you are doing to others. You don't need their judgment. Just follow the directions now. It's over! ».

Something worthy living for

The cigarette indicates low inner energy. It is not a question of age, but of purpose and motivation. Mrs Mary, an 85-year-old granny, seemed to have no reason to move on. Jack, the grandson who had quit smoking with my support, wanted at all costs to try to help his grandmother to quit too. But often, the more one gets older, the less motivation has, at least as regards the possibility of throwing out the cigarette. However, in order to eliminate the addiction to smoking and transform it, as in our case, into energy that produces a result for our benefit, the active person's participation is necessary.

Grandmother Mary had, among other things, a serious discomfort: she had been living in a wheelchair for about 10 years. It was probably not the best situation to quit smoking, do you agree with me? Anyway, given Jack's insistence, I went to visit her at home to meet her and have a chat. On the one hand, I kept asking myself: «What can I say to a person who has been in a wheelchair for 10 years? And you that you are 85 years old? What motivations could she have?» On the other hand, I felt pleasantly involved because I had a great bond with my grandparents, so the idea of being able to help Mary made me feel good, it satisfied me. When I met her and introduced myself, she looked bewildered, and even a little annoyed. She knew what I was doing and why I went to visit her. Although it is usually difficult to dissuade me from my intentions, her attitude was clear: her grandmother Mary did not have the same purpose at all. I asked her what she was going to do tonight. She replied: «The usual things. Now what can I do at my age, and in these conditions? ». There was a mixture of sadness, anger and resignation in her words. And I understood her. «What will she do in the next few days?» I asked her again. «Dear!», She told me «now my life is in this chair and nothing more». At that very moment, I understood how important it is to have a goal that keeps us motivated. Thinking about all this I asked my resigned granny how she saw herself in the next 5 years. «5 years!» she replied:

«I will not be there anymore!». «And if there was, what would she be like?» «I don't see myself, what should I do so combined?» Granny could no longer imagine her future. You must know that those who suffer from an addiction (*that is not the cause but the symptom, remember it*) cannot imagine her future, or at least he does not see it rosy. Addictions are an elegant way to commit suicide. And smoking seems to be among the most sought after. The smoker goes towards a future that he does not see, it is as if he were going to die; and on the other hand, smoking helps him get there faster. The present becomes a real suffering. The smoker suffers terribly in the present. All dark, all gone. He finds no loopholes, nothing. Living in a present without a future is like being in a 1m x 1m room and walking on a treadmill. And opening that single window you can see a brick wall. There is no air at the mere thought!

There is always a way out. This is our job, to look at reality with different eyes.

By smoking a deep belief that the next cigarette will change is created. However, it never happens. Smoking is the manifestation of the impossibility of changing one's life. Maybe you have tried it, so you know what I mean. With each cigarette, hopefully for something different. Then, you always find yourself in the same room leading the same life. But as impossible as it may seem to get out, all rooms have doors. You can continue to believe that someone else has locked you in or recognize that you have the key in your pocket. Now stop! Take that key, put it in the lock, open it and go out to live your life.

Grandmother Mary had also abandoned the rituals. Rituals are very important. They allow us to mark the path, they define life. They orient us. They tell us where we are, how much time has passed and how much we still have ahead of us. Those who do not have rituals without a scan of the time that passes, of the before, during and after. Those who have too many clings to an imaginary life. The ritual, when it is healthy, marks a stage in a path: the silver and then gold wedding anniversary, the party for the 18 years, for the 30 and then again for the 50, Christmas, the harvest in autumn, the monthly salary, weekly shopping, daily training, lunch, dinner... And all the other big or small events, that mark our existence. The cigarette, on the other hand, is an obsessive ritual. The smoker who replaces healthy rituals with smoking becomes more and more convinced that with each cigarette he advances one step in his life path, but he walks on that treadmill. He stands still within four walls.

Think about how you will be in 5, 10, 20, 30 years...

_____

_____

_____

Think about what you will be like and what you will do.

_____

_____

_____

Think about how you will be at your best.

_____

_____

_____

Think of the best for you and your family.

_____

_____

_____

And now act! Start improving your life now. Act against any unfavourable data. It is important for you to understand that "not doing" is the antechamber of failure, of death. Making, even if it involves inconveniences, difficulties, mistakes can be pleasant and motivating and is the anticipation of "personal success". And grandma Mary? As I anticipated, I did not go further, I limited myself to that conversation. It was a pleasant acquaintance. However, before I left, I asked the family a few questions. A great motivation was needed, a great joy. What makes a difference in people's lives is that there is something worth living for. A few months later Jack called me all enthusiastic: «My grandmother doesn't smoke anymore; she threw the packet in front of me, and she cried with joy when I told her that she will have another granddaughter!»

Despite her inner suffering, Grandma Mary now had a new perspective, someone to pass on a part of herself. I think that leaving a part of us is, right up to the end, the greatest motivation. Here's how it works: Learn to project yourself into your future and you will be free. Live the present according to your vision. Who smokes is resigned!

It all depends on how you perceive and construct reality in your mind. Granny Mary could have been disheartened once again, thinking negatively that she would never see her granddaughter growing up. Instead, she reacted with a proactive attitude. It means that the event was the input, but then it was she who chose which life to live. Events can be a stimulus, but you do the rest. The point is not how long you have left to live, but *how* you decide to live it. Indeed, just to be honest, you should not even wait for an external stimulus to change, because you choose which life to live. On the other hand, it could also be that you had a thousand incentives to live a peaceful, full and happy life, but you have not grasped them. When one is in a state of mental and emotional numbness, one does not have the full capacity to see reality.

Regardless, take your life in hand, step out of the room that keeps you trapped and live the life you want. Be unreasonable. Go out and change the patterns. Build it against everything and everyone if that is the case. Create the optimal environment for your dreams to come true. Nothing and no one will ever decide for you, least of all the cigarette. Now, there is you and what is worth living for!

Thanks, but I don't smoke!

You should know that, in order to test the effectiveness of the book, I had some people read it and they gave me important feedback. My concern, not being in direct contact with them, was not being able to give the desired and effective imprinting. Luckily, I was wrong and after some corrections to the work you are reading, the feedback was: "You have entered my mind and I can no longer think about it. I forgot how I was before, now I am a non-smoker. I hear your voice telling me that I can do it, that I am great and when I think about the cigarette, I feel nausea first, and then the image of myself and my splendid future appears; I love myself and I do everything to feel good, I am the master of my life. I decide!"

By reading this book you will install new files in your mind and an internal supervisor who will control you and direct you towards wellness by feeding yourself. This is the automatic mechanism of successful people: an automatic mechanism that pushes towards well-being. When you do something to improve, and deal with a change, a thousand resistances can trigger, thoughts like: "What am I doing?", "I will never stop", "It's just a matter of will!", "These are just bullshit", "I can't find any improvement", "If I want to, I stop all by myself", etc. This is the conditioned mind trying to sabotage our work together, do not listen to it! Remember instead that I am always there to be your supporter, fan and coach and that you can do it, even to tell your mind: "Thanks, but I don't smoke!"

Exercise

From now on you have a very simple task to do. Do you want to know what it is? When you have the desire to light a cigarette, first make sure it is a strong desire. If it isn't, forget it.

Figure 5

Wait until the critical moment comes back. As soon as you are there to take the cigarette between your fingers... stop! Block everything, the movie that is all the mental projections associated with the cigarette and the sensations. Press the thumb and forefinger of your right hand (PIDX) together and repeat to your mind: "Thank you, I don't smoke!"

From now on, whenever you desire a cigarette, say "stop"!

I also invite you to think about another aspect: many smokers spend a considerable amount of their money on cigarettes, from one thousand to three thousand euros a year. Probably some of you also fall into this range. Many of them have bills and car insurance to pay; some barely put food on the table, otherwise, they continue to smoke; still others would like to change their car, take a vacation, renew their wardrobe and often just do it. Nobody thinks that getting rid of the cigarette would mean having the possibility, even economic, to fulfil some wishes. Investing in cigarettes is a guarantee to harm yourself. Spend your money to get worse... Wow! I make you a proposal: you pay me half of what you spend on cigarettes, and I promise to make you feel bad. Would you like to pay me to feel bad? I do not think so at all!

Repeat aloud:

"I don't want to spend money to feel bad anymore!"

Repeat this by looking in the mirror 5 more times.

If you continue to smoke, let me ask you a question: what perfume do you use? How much it costs? Why are you wearing it? So, why do you smoke? Maybe you are one of those who chew gum after smoking? Do you think that a chewing gum can purify the air in the lungs and around you?

Maybe they will invent such a tire sooner or later but know that now it does not exist. It means you stink! And I assure you that whoever approaches you thinks: "What a disgust, you can't be near you!". These are not my personal comments, but those of your former smoking colleagues.

Start postponing now, telling yourself:

"Thanks, I don't smoke!"

Remember to press PIDX every time you repeat it.

It will help you.

The Angel and the Demon

Each of us has two guests inside, an angel and a demon, who whisper in our ears what and how to do. Your addict is run by a demon, who pushes you to make a morbid bond with people or to bond with cigarettes and other drugs. When you are unable to live without a bond, the latter becomes harmful, it turns into a prison: the smoker is a slave to cigarettes, he cannot be without it. It must be repeated, however, that addiction is not something negative regardless: it is part of life itself, of the survival of each of us. At certain stages it is even necessary, as in the relationship between mother and child. However, if it persists and does not evolve into independence, it can be very harmful. Thus, the relationship with the cigarette does not make you grow and harms you. It does not last for a limited time; it is often forever. The child needs a relationship of dependence because he cannot alone, but you can provide for yourself. Or am I wrong?

On the contrary, a free person, as the word itself suggests, is not dependent, not tied up. Being free does not mean having relationships, not feeling affection for others, not caring about the people you love; rather, it means loving oneself above all else, respecting oneself, feeling good about oneself even more than with others, feeling complete, fulfilled. When a person has learned to feel good about himself, he is able to attract and create healthy and empowering relationships, avoiding the harmful ones. The smoker, on the other hand, does not know how to be alone and chooses the cigarette as "company". Learning to feel good about yourself has a double advantage: it helps not only to avoid the harmful relationship with the cigarette, but also to establish relationships of wellness with others. Moreover, the demon takes over and drains vital energy to a minimum: life seems like a prison, one feels crushed and oppressed by limiting beliefs about oneself and the external environment and the lack of an attractive perspective. The cause of one's difficulties is continually sought in others, in the external world or in the relationship with the transcendent. In any case, an innocent person is put in jail, while the real culprit is around to commit a crime. The culprit, the demon, has a name and it is called attachment.

I repeat, in the early stages of an individual's life it has an evolutionary purpose: it is necessary as nourishment and growth until the transition to maturity, to adulthood in which one takes care of oneself independently. This is a critical step for everyone. Those who fail resists by attaching themselves to anything. Eliminating attachment means freeing yourself, loving yourself and loving without constraints, feelings of guilt, fears, anger, frustration and sadness. In order to cling tooth and nail to situations, relationships and people, to work itself, to money, as well as to certain ideas about material goods and their possession, is not freedom. Many people believe they are free because they despise material possessions and take refuge in the spiritual sphere, or because they do not have much money and then criticize the material wealth in others. It is still a form of attachment. Everything that is attachment is pathologic or, it is negative.

In the balance we can find freedom

Creating harmony in your life is freedom. Loving another person and perceiving freedom. Doing a job and feeling the freedom. Wanting to lose weight and feeling freedom. Quit smoking and feeling free. Whatever you do, it is important that you feel the sense of freedom. If not, you are feeding attachment, your prison. Freedom is your angel!

The intention to change

How important is it for you to change your situation? Why?

_____

_____

_____

What would you lose and what would you gain by freeing yourself from smoking now?

_____

_____

_____

What are you willing to do from now to permanently change? What are you willing to give up?

_____

_____

_____

What is the worst thing that could happen to you getting rid of the cigarette, then changing?

_____

By freeing yourself from the cigarette, by making this change, what improvements would you get?

Rereading the answers, how do you feel about the possibility of a real change in your life? What about being able to be a non-smoker again, yourself again?

The past

How and who were you before you started smoking?

What are the differences between who you were when you were not smoking and who you are today?

___

The present

What aspect would you recover from your past, where you were a non-smoker, which would improve you today?

___

What aspect of yourself today that you do not like would you replace him with?

___

The future

If you decide to get rid of the cigarette today, how could you be different tomorrow? Why?

___

_____

_____

What could you integrate into the present of what you like about the idea of your future?

_____

_____

_____

Summarize the several items: make a summary of the answers. Read them again before moving on. Then, divide the contents into the past, present and future: "I did, and I thought... from now on I think and do... I will do and I will be...".

_____

_____

_____

Your motivation

Indicate your degree of motivation to free yourself from smoking. Colour the squares from left to right:

1									10

Maybe you have been motivated in the past, or you are motivated even now, but you still cannot get rid of it completely. I understand you. Do your children tell you to stop? Do the morning cough and the sense of discomfort in moments of physical fatigue put you to the test? Do you smell like smoke and your partner cannot stand it anymore? Is it late, out of cigarettes and you must get up and go buy them in the middle of the night? These and who knows how many other reasons smokers must quit, and maybe they are yours too.

The main difficulty is that, at the same time, the smoker also has reasons to continue smoking. In fact, the smoker feels physical discomfort, abstinence, and a psychological and emotional discomfort that prompt him to look for a cigarette. Thus a "conflict" is triggered. It is the conflict that creates discomfort and makes one feel bad. You know the tug of war? What was done in the summer camps between two teams? Imagine this rope, you in the middle being pulled from one side and the other. You want to quit, you want to be free from smoking once and for all but, at the same time, you also want to "relax", thanks to the cigarette, you want to "overcome a relational discomfort" thanks to the cigarette, you want to "do your job well" thanks to the cigarette, you want "to pass quickly the time that you do not like" thanks to the cigarette, you want to overcome a "frustration, a rejection, a pain, a suffering" thanks to the cigarette, and you want to face much more that makes you feel bad, thanks to it. You want to spend an evening "in company" thanks to the cigarette. How many times have I heard: "He keeps me company!". Oh are you sure? "Can you talk to us with your cigarette?", I usually reply. On the one hand, you are motivated to quit for several reasons, on the other hand, to continue smoking for others. You run the risk of coming out of this dispute with broken bones. There are those who remain bogged down all their lives doing nothing, putting off, inventing a thousand excuses. On the other hand, there are those who clumsily try to quit, without succeeding and thus ending up demoralized.

Increase your motivation

The reason that pushes you to do or not to do an action is almost never just one.

Perhaps it will be a thought that will make you take a certain decision rather than another, like the straw that breaks the camel's back. At the same time, it is not the last straw, but it is all the others that are inside the jar that make the difference. Fill your motivational jar with all the good reasons you find.

Add up the A's and C's that fill your jar. Write down all the benefits on a separate sheet that you will always keep with you, so that when others come to mind you can insert them. Write down the disadvantages on another sheet. Done? Well.

Keep smoking		Free from cigarette	
Advantages	Disadvantages	Advantages	Disadvantages
It helps me to relax	I spend too much every month	I breath perfectly	Discomfort in the gestures

Now, burn this second sheet with a match. Do exactly what I tell you. Repeat this last exercise as often as you feel the need, it helps to eliminate harmful residues. You can also do this with all the negative thoughts that sometimes cross your mind. It's great exercise. It works. The most important thing for you is to keep the benefits in mind and heart. Always carry the benefits sheet with you. Read it at least once a day. If possible, keep it in the pocket near the heart. I am not joking, really do it.

Your goal

Answer this question, be specific: what is the result you would like to achieve at the end of this book? "Losing weight" or "losing 4 kg" are not good, they are not goals. In order to be motivating, the goal must be formulated in positive, specific and attractive terms. For example: "I see myself with a lean physique, sculpted abdomen and attract women" and start dieting and training; "I have recovered in excellent physical shape, and I enjoy life with my children" and throw away your cigarettes, eat well and do what you need. If formulated in these terms, the goal is clear, attractive and guides you to achieve it. Find your goal without the cigarette, start a new non-smoking life:

_____

_____

_____

How do you intend to achieve this? Example: going to the gym, following a healthy diet and a targeted program.

_____

_____

_____

How long will it take? What do you need to achieve it? Capacities - Skills - Means.

_____

_____

_____

Answering will not be immediately easy, in any case, commit yourself and think about it. Even if you find immediate answers, return to them daily to assimilate them and see that they are the most suitable for you. You can change the answers as you become more self-aware. Start off on other roads, create opportunities where there were none before or you didn't see any. Activate the mechanism of change.

Now answer the question: What is important to you now, in life? Ex: *family, love, affections, work, etc.* Indicate all the values that distinguish you and write the reason why for each one. Write your list:

_____

_____

_____

Which of these values and how does continuing to smoke contradict, or could it be?

_____

_____

_____

Getting rid of cigarettes, becoming a non-smoker, which of these values do you agree with and why?

_____

_____

_____

Indicate your degree of motivation to free yourself from the cigarette now.

1									10

The great evil heals the little one

You have often heard this oriental adage. This scheme has a great impact on people's lives. Even on yours. We humans could self-manipulate and tell us the stories that are most useful to us in order to "live" and face everyday life. The idea that the great evil heals the little one comes to our rescue when we find ourselves having to face hard, sometimes dramatic situations. For example, a bruise on a sore arm fades into the background if you break your leg. So, the lesser evil disappears, it seems "healed". The meaning is this. The evils become two, no longer one.

Our mind focuses on the biggest, heaviest and most dramatic problem - sometimes even just imaginary - and immediately the "lesser" evil is attenuated. Many people use this strategy to "live" their life. Sentences such as "I could have been worse, and in this condition I'm fine" or the classic "I smoke but I don't take drugs" or "I smoke but I have no other vices" are typical of those who try to demonstrate an alleged advantage over to a situation - even if only hypothetical - far worse. Or they take others by comparison: "Look at the one who has never smoked and died of a heart attack!". And many other useless and out of place statements.

It is important to stay focused on yourself. When you turn the conversation to others you are not developing your potential, you are justifying your failures. If you really want to make comparisons, take an example from people full of energy and wellness. They love and treat their body well, respect each other. Compare yourself with those who are well to get ideas, suggestions and motivation. Observing who has made it, who is able to lead a satisfying life, helps to think that yes, it is possible... and that the time has come to get a move on! Comparing or dating people who are worse off than us undoubtedly reduces the sense of personal frustration. Yet the smartest and most useful thing that can be done is to watch and take an example from successful people, even if it can generate further frustration because it reminds us that it is necessary to imp care to make a difference. In fact, a common reaction is to belittle the success of others by labelling it as "luck". Can you think of someone you know?

When your mind begins to justify situations that you live inside with a feeling of discomfort, then stop and listen to yourself first. If a certain situation makes you feel bad, it does not make you live well but, despite everything, you tend to stay there, to repeat it over time, it is very likely that even you are victims of the mechanism according to which the great evil cures the small evil and that to warn your life as pleasant and just, you tend to compare yourself with situations of greater malaise so that your little daily malaise can be passed off as "positive". This is the alibi that often acts when you smoke. The feeling of "pleasure" is not real, it is just less pain; however, your mind likes to call it "pleasure" to distort perception, as a matter of survival. Do you want to know how to avoid falling into this pattern? "Raise your standards". Yes, I mean: "Stop playing humble falsehoods." Take your life in order to live it fully. Expect the best in everything you do. You deserve it. If you do not do it, no one will ever do it for you. Not because there are no good people, but because those around you exist to confirm the opinion you have of yourself. If you demand the best for yourself, even those around you will recognize it. Face your difficulties face to face, do not evade them by confronting them with even bigger problems, which then all come together. The moments of discomfort, of difficulty must be faced, not avoided!

Your health gains

A whole other world. Many say to me: "I look back and say to myself: was that me?". Everything changes:

- "I'm more beautiful".
- "My skin has improved, much better than the more expensive cream".
- "My daughter told me that she loves me because I don't smoke anymore".
- "My father is proud of me; he had never told me before".
- "I breathe freely without worries, I have resumed freediving and running".
- "I have lost weight, I feel better about myself, I play sports that I did not like before".
- "I was taking medications to regulate blood pressure. Before, I halved them and now I don't take them anymore".
- "I don't cough anymore; I have no phlegm and I like it when they tell me I smell good. Before they hardly ever told me".
- "I have improved in sport and I feel appreciated".
- "I went on a trip with my wife, which I haven't done for a long time".

- "I feel free, and I choose for myself".

- "I'm as strong as before, I still can't believe it. I took my life back in my hand ".

Speaking of the harms of smoking, I tried to limit myself because I think psychological terrorism is useless and does not generate motivation. The data below are taken from the Ministry of Health website20 and indicate the benefits and improvements that are obtained over time after quitting smoking. This is motivating!

Within 20 Minutes

- Blood pressure normalizes

- Heart rate normalizes

- The temperature of the hands and feet returns to normal within 8 hours

- The level of carbon monoxide in the blood drops

- Blood oxygen levels normalize within 24 hours

- Decreases the risk of heart attack

Within 48 Hours

- Nerve endings begin to grow back

- They improve the senses of smell and taste within 72 hours

- The bronchi relax, breathing improves

- Lung capacity increases

From 2 weeks to 3 months

- Improves circulation

---

[20] Ministero della Salute, "10 buoni motivi per smettere di fumare", 30/05/2013: http://www.salute.gov.it/portale/temi/p2_6.jsp?lingua=italiano&id=465&area=stiliVita&menu=fumo

- Walking becomes increasingly less tiring

- The ciliated epithelium of the respiratory tract, destroyed by smoke, grows back and the impurities inside the airways are expelled from 3 to 9 months

- Fatigue, shortness of breath and other symptoms, such as cough, decrease

- Increase your overall energy level

Within 5 Years

- Lung cancer mortality for the average smoker (one pack of cigarettes a day) drops from 137 to 72 for every hundred thousand people

Within 10 Years

- Precancerous cells are replaced

- Decreases the risk of other cancers: in the mouth, larynx, oesophagus, bladder, kidneys and pancreas after 15 years

- Lung cancer mortality drops to 12 per hundred thousand which is normal; practically the risk of dying from lung cancer is comparable to that of a person who has never smoked.

In the early days, like a baby who is born and filling his lungs with air he cries for the first time, you will feel some discomfort that will also be a sign of a new life. If you have already tried to quit in the past, you know what I mean: increased expectoration, disorientation, numbness of the muscles, increased appetite, stomach cramps, sweating, etc. Each of these symptoms will give you the dimension of the cleansing process taking place. Expectorating will allow you to throw out the residual mucus and get rid of it; stomach cramps will tell you that nicotine is leaving your body, or rather, they are a manifestation of withdrawal, as are muscle numbness, sweating and tremors. Getting rid of smoke, you will perceive smells better, consequently you will taste better and experience more pleasure in food. I give these examples to make you understand that any discomfort you may experience will be a sign of improvement. It will not last long, it is only the first few weeks. Break free now. You will have a thousand rewards immediately. The advantage will be your well-being at 360 °. The "non-smokers" live better, because they find a feeling of energy. And they go to great lengths to make it a new good habit. Habit is in our nature. We are habitual. Choose to be towards well-being, rather than towards malaise.

Think - Feel - Act differently!

You will get powerful new results! When you buy a new car, you have the best intentions. You treat it as if it were your own daughter. Make sure it is always clean, and that makes you feel good. Over time, some begin to pay less attention to it, they do not take it to wash as often, they dirty and neglect it. Each of us treats his car as he wishes, but no one would ever be so stupid as to put dirty petrol in it with the risk of damaging the engine. Would you do it? No, absolutely no. Yet that is what you do to your body if you smoke. Put dirty gasoline. As indicated by an American study on treatment4addiction. Like 21 any cigarette smoked, it is equivalent to 13.8 minutes less life for a smoker. According to the same study, a smoker lives up to 69 years on average, 10 years less than a non-smoker.

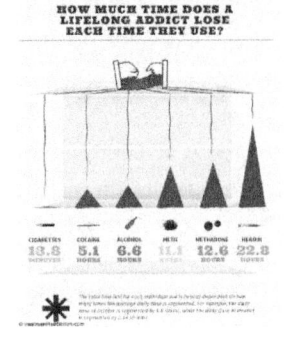

Figure 6

1. How many years of life have you lost:
Years of smoking n. .... years × n. Mr. daily ....
(e.g. 20) × 365 = ... (smoked cigarettes) × 13.8 minutes = ... /525.600 (minutes contained in one year) = (...................)
2. How many years of life will you lose if you continue to smoke: (80 - your age .... years) = ... years × n . Mr. daily .... (ex.: 20) × 365 = ... (cigarettes smoked) × 13.8 minutes = ... /525.600 = ...

---

21 G. Ciucci, "Una sigaretta ti toglie 14 minuti di vita, un drink quasi 7 ore", lo studio pubblicato dal sito treatment4addiction.com, «Huffington Post». http://www.huffingtonpost.it/2014/10/14/sigaretta-14-minuti_n_5981488.html

Economic management

From the first day you quit smoking, put the exact amount you spent on cigarettes aside in a jar. At the end of the month, take the total amount and divide it into two parts. You must - and I repeat *you must* - spend part of it for yourself, for your entertainment: a weekend in the mountains, a trip, a special gift, a gallant dinner, in short, whatever you want and like. But not to pay the fine you got - you should pay this anyway. The other half donates it to charity. After the entertainment that many deprive themselves, having a high sense of duty, what will make you grow and evolve more as an individual is to help others. Many of my friends and clients have experienced the wellness and joy that come from helping others with the same money that would otherwise have gone up in smoke, as well as threatening health. Even today, years after the cessation, they continue to do so. They told me: "Helping others was the incentive, the greatest gratification that gave meaning and meaning to everything". I often suggest long distance adoption, or the simple act of shopping for those in need or helping some young people in their studies. This is perhaps the biggest secret of people who have managed to improve themselves and enter a new perspective of well-being, and now it is you who can use it to your advantage. This economic habit educates people to consider themselves important, to become better people. He teaches to create a balance thinking also of others as well as of themselves, giving help to those who do not have the same opportunities as us and to those who have not yet understood what and how to improve themselves. We have a moral obligation to these people and supporting them helps us to evolve and become better. A better person doesn't smoke. Smoking is not part of her habits, so it is not part of your new habits either.

Self-representation

In my daily experience, I notice that those who experience hardships in their lives in most cases have a distorted and inappropriate idea of their identity, or rather confuse it with social roles or fail to distinguish between them. Each of us lives several lives in one. He is a parent, athlete, partner, friend, entrepreneur, partner, colleague, child, etc. Each of us is many people in one. Depending on the context, one should adapt.

Of course, without becoming depersonalized, I take it for granted. This is a sign of balance, of sanity. Often, however, the vision of one's identity crystallizes, and dysfunctional relationships arise in which, instead of changing one's role based on the context - which can change several times in the same day - one becomes rigid and generalizes a certain role to all areas. of life. Thus relational difficulties arise with the surrounding environment. Fabio is an excellent soldier. Highly decorated for his heroic deeds and the commitment shown in the mission. Thanks to him, dozens of soldiers have returned to their families. Probably one of the best soldiers of the last fifty years. His martial attitude, discipline and rigor have enabled him to save hundreds of lives. The right person at the right time. Honour to merit. Fabio, back home, relates to his wife and his two daughters in the same way he manages his men. Although animated by his best intentions, Fabio "takes off his uniform", but continues to be a soldier even at home. What do you think comes out of it?

A disaster. Why? At home you are companions, husbands, fathers and you must express these parts of you, of your identity, for the good and happiness of all. The same confusion is also created with *emotions* and *moods*: "I am angry" or "I am depressed" and many other idioms. Those who have the tendency, indeed the habit of exchanging their identity with an emotion, especially if "negative", recognize themselves in that, and others also end up identifying them with that emotion or state of mind. When you often repeat "*I am* nervous" instead of "I feel nervous", this state of mind becomes your identity, and you will do everything to be so.

In addition to emotions and moods, we often tend to mistakenly identify ourselves with a single behaviour. "I behave well, I pay taxes I don't steal, the same: I'm a good person". Again, that is not quite the case. It is a behaviour, not an identity. A behaviour does not make a person's identity, just as those who are starving and steal a sandwich as the only resource should not be labelled as a thief. He is just a person in great difficulty who has not found a better solution at the time. That does not make him a bad person, at least to me. Who am I to judge from behaviour? I would like to see how many "good people" in the same situation would remain so. Understand that a behaviour is a behaviour, nothing else.

I often hear smokers say: "I am a smoker... and I don't want to quit, I am a smoker and I like it, etc." and other similar sentences. The Orientals consider the word as living, for them the word has a soul. It can change the external world and the internal one of each of us. If you say, "I am a smoker", you are just basing your identity on smoking, and by doing so you condition every cell of your body in that direction, to the extent that you believe in it and repeat it every day to yourself and to others. What does it mean to transform a specific action into one's identity? If the action becomes identity:

1. I will have to repeat the behaviour in order to recognize myself, allowing others to recognize me. Because it is my identity, my nature, my way of being. Even if this behaviour is harmful as is the cigarette, I will be forced to repeat it to recognize me and be recognized, because denying one's identity would be tantamount to killing an important part of oneself.

2. I will live in a state of perennial tension due to the "must". If the smoker's identity is linked to a behaviour, the smoker to exist as such must absolutely repeat the gesture even if he hurts him, even if he does not want to. Those who get trapped inside this mechanism waste great energy and there are few times when they can relax and really be themselves.

The first part of the sentence – "I am a smoker" - is very powerful as it affirms an identity and therefore becomes real. The second part of the sentence "... I like it" is a justification, a defence of the mind. Yes, your mind protects you, it knows that you would never do anything against your person, so create an alibi so that you too can believe it and continue with the harmful behaviour. It is truly amazing what our mind can do!

Identity: I am a smoker.

Justification: I like it; I have no other vices; I don't want to stop...

If you want to free yourself from smoking, the smartest formula you could use to describe yourself is: "I smoke cigarettes", "I smoked a cigarette" and the like. It is important and useful to remain focused solely on the behaviour. If it occurs to you to think or say that "you are a smoker", stop the thought for a moment, rephrase the sentence and refer to the behaviour: "I smoke cigarettes" instead of "I am a smoker". Similarly, to the question "Are you a smoker?" The most useful answer is "No, I smoke cigarettes". Because by doing so you present smoking in your eyes and others in terms of behaviour and no longer as an uncomfortable and unproductive identity to be strengthened. Since the behaviour is much easier to eliminate, do you understand now why I am making you think in these terms?

Exercise

I am .... (write your name) and smoke cigarettes.

Repeat this 5 times, even if you have already stopped.

> Now do this exercise. First, repeat the wrong statement. Write here the wrong statement three times:
>
> I am a smoker of (n. Mr.) per day ....
>
> Now write:
>
> I am (name) and I smoke (no. Mr.) at the day ....
>
> Take a red marker, the kind with a thick tip that leave a mark on the back of the paper and put an X over the wrong statement. From now on you are yourself, and what keeps you tied to the cigarette is just behaviour. You have now recovered and cleared your identity. Repeat and write the third statement 5 times.

Whether you already feel free from smoking or feel the need to take some more time, before moving on to the next chapter get used to recognizing your identity with your name and, when you refer to the habit of smoking, speak of a behaviour and no more as your identity. It never was. By doing so, you will strengthen your identity. The smoker has a low opinion of himself, as I said in the introduction, and you will regain some of your personal power with this exercise, which will be useful to you always and everywhere.

Advantages of change

What are the positive aspects of being a non-smoker?

_____

_____

_____

If you had the last wish of Aladdin's lamp available to change your life, how would you like it to be from now on?

_____

_____

What are the positive aspects of making a change at this moment in your life?

What makes you believe that if you decide to free yourself from the cigarette, you will be able to quit?

In what past situation did you successfully make a big change, and maybe you thought you were not capable of it?

How did you do? What did you tell yourself? What beliefs drove you: about yourself, about others, about circumstances?

_____

_____

How and when did you realize you could do it?

_____

_____

_____

How can you use this experience now?

_____

_____

_____

Enter K +

Your state of strength

We enter the K+ state. So called in NLP (Neuro Linguistic Programming), it is the state that athletes define Zone, the state of maximum performance, or in any case of high performance. Marc, a man in his forties, led a life that others had chosen for him and, for this reason, he had lost a lot of his energy: he was unmotivated, unmade, he did not want to commit. I order to encourage him, I suggested this exercise: «Close your eyes and breathe deeply, take a few minutes just for yourself. You don't necessarily have to remember a specific moment, even a vague memory or feeling alone is fine. A moment, a period of your life when you knew you were in this state of strength. Now, travel into the past, as if you were walking backwards in time until the moment you felt strong; it doesn't matter how far you walk - even to the womb, it doesn't matter - but I want it to be your best time. As soon as you return to that moment, you will feel a great energy flood your body and light up with your favourite colour».

> **Exercise**
>
> I want you to also think about a situation in your past where you have experienced happiness and wellness. A moment when you felt strong, effective and responsive.
>
> When you enter the coloured light, push your thumb against the index finger of the right hand (PIDX) and focus on the positive sensations.
>
> Now return walking towards the present moment, bring the light and all the sensations of inner strength, well-being and happiness with you; colour your timeline so far.
>
> Repeat the exercise 5 times.
>
> Now that you have learned to enter your state of strength, breathe deeply and press the fingers of your right hand, and repeat 3 times aloud:
>
> "I am greater than any difficulty!"

Amplify the energy

Exercise

> 1. Visualize a spark of energy within you; you can do this with your eyes closed, or by leaving them open and gazing at a point in space.
>
> 2. Now the spark is getting even bigger, expanding until it becomes greater than you. You are enveloped in this energy as in a bubble that nourishes you. You feel good, the more it envelops you, the more it grows and expands, until it becomes so big as to invest everything around you; you are getting increasingly bigger. As big as your city, as big as your nation, as big as the world, even bigger. You feel great, wider than any obstacle or difficulty. Smile. You become a little more aware of your body and the feelings of well-being it gives you with each breath you take.
> *Continue to press the fingers of the right hand against each other.*
>
> 3. Slowly come back into yourself to an energy level that maintains that feeling of well-being and strength that you now know.

Return to this chapter whenever you feel the need to re-charge the batteries. Consider that you are used this exercise to tell yourself the worst things, treating yourself badly like you would not allow anyone, you have been doing it for a long time now. You must repeat this exercise repeatedly, it requires a lot of training. Remember that you can now access your strength state whenever you want, at any time.

Centring

What is that? It is the feeling of inner stability and balance. One is centred in a state of wellness. But what does centring have to do with quitting smoking? Let's see it.

Exercise

1. Now stand up and rate your current centred state from 1 to 10. How do you feel?

Breathe slowly and go deeper and deeper with your own breath, as in a daydream; keep breathing and descending. While standing, focus on the feeling of stability and rate it from 1 to 10. Observe and visualize the grade.

2. Now, a very thin thread of light of your favourite colour enters the centre of your head from above, crosses your entire body and descends until it enters the earth and from there towards infinity. From your right, another very thin thread of light enters your side, just below the navel, crosses the centre of your body and extends towards infinity, on the other side. The two threads come together in the centre and are *indissolubly* combined, they are welded while other threads of light, of the most beautiful and colourful, begin to cross you in all directions, binding all together in the centre, and then extend towards infinity. Meanwhile, continue to breathe deeply, feet firm and stable. Press forefinger and thumb of your right hand (PIDX).

Repeat 5 times.

From 1 to 10, how centred do you feel? Has the value increased then before? If so, you have done the exercise well.

> Otherwise repeat it again. The more you practice this exercise, the more you will raise the level of experience.

Create the optimal environment

The surrounding environment, what is outside us, should not be underestimated, but not overestimated either. In fact, we are influenced but, at the same time, we can influence ourselves and the environment in which we live. It is therefore important to create an empowering inner environment and a supportive outer environment. How to do? Here are some tips to follow.

Be centred

When we put aside our desires, we are not centred. You must think hard about your desire and set it as your goal. Without becoming a source of stress, but of motivation. Move towards your purposes, live the life you want. Not the "must" one!

Be aligned

When mind, body and spirit are not in harmony with each other, we are not aligned. This happens when, due to several reasons, we focus only on one aspect neglecting the others. Make your mind and body feel good. It is unbalanced to focus obsessively on work without ever taking a moment for yourself, or to look after your physical shape without thinking about the state of health of thoughts and the quality of relationships. Your spiritual side is something that transcends you, that you strive for. A source of inspiration. We have clarity only when mind and body develop together.

Power

Having great energy does not simply mean "feeling fit". It means having that inner strength that nothing can scratch judgments, insults, or other. Energy attracts the same frequencies to itself, remember that. The surrounding environment is a symptom of your energy. If there is a good, proactive, empowering environment around you, it means that your energy is high. What environment do you have around you? Would you like to change it? Increase your energy.

Empowering beliefs

"I am able to get, do, be what I want. What is right for me. What you want or. I know I have to improve and learn new skills to achieve my goals, and I can do it". List the skills you want to achieve:

_____

_____

_____

Mental attitude

Loving yourself despite everything is a key aspect. The more you enter this perspective, the more your mood and relationships with others will change. The more we love each other, always and in any case, the more we activate things, situations and people that improve us.

Feeling deserving

People's main problem is not feeling deserving of the best. I know it may sound strange, but I can assure you: it is true. Most of the people I follow in coaching have this common belief: "they don't feel deserving of the best". Even if on a conscious level we have a goal - for example to make a career, have a family, a beautiful home - we can unwittingly harbour the deep conviction that we do not deserve all of this. There are several reasons, which however have roots in our personal history. In order to overcome this limitation, it is important to anticipate it and focus on the goal and what it will entail having achieved it. How will you feel once you have reached your goal? How would you feel free from the cigarette? Do you feel you deserve to be healthy?

_____

_____

_____

Behaviour

Action, result, learning, new action. Follow this pattern, it can be applied to everything. First act (off the cigarettes), then observe the result, learn something about yourself and take a new action until the improvement and the result. Continue following all the points.

Commit yourself to your personal success, be free, strong people, full of energy, make sure that your life is full of love and wellness. Learn from your past and make the best of it. Live the period of liberation from the cigarette aware of the need to create a balance between "wellness" and "discomfort".

You cannot hope to be able to achieve your goals without bothering yourself and shaking up the existing situation. If this were not the case, there would be no improvement. The main reason many people do not evolve is that they fear discomfort and therefore go to great lengths in order to avoid them. But the whole is a unity formed by the set of several parts. Therefore, to create unity, it takes good and evil, black and white, etc. Do everything with balance: everything is useful for another. If you avoid an extreme, you will experience a state of imbalance. You cannot think that you are fine by avoiding discomfort! Strive to build the future you want, even if this can be a cause for temporary discomfort in the present. Accept that moment of discomfort necessary to build your future, while learning to enjoy the progress you have made in the present. It is all a question of balance. Dream, think, create for yourself an attractive future. You can do it.

A new environment of wellness

Further confirmation of the need to create an environment of well-being around oneself to free oneself from the addiction to cigarettes always comes from the same article by Johann Hari on the "mouse park" experiment. We already know that mice that live in an optimal environment avoid doped water, even though they have tasted it in the past. Hari continues[22]:

---

22 J. Hari, op. cit.

«At first, I thought it was just a strange thing about mice, until I discovered that - in the same period as the "mouse park" experiment - there was its human equivalent. It was called the Vietnam War. Vime magazine wrote that heroin use was "as common as chewing gum" among American soldiers, and that there was concrete evidence: according to research published in the Archives of General Psychiatry, about 20 percent some American soldiers in that country had become addicted to heroin. Many felt understandably terrified; convinced that at the end of the war a huge number of drug addicts would return to their homeland. The truth is that about 95 percent of those who developed that addiction - according to the same research - simply did not take drugs afterwards. Few were forced to rehabilitate. The fact is that they had gone from a terrifying cage to a pleasant one, so they stopped yearning for drugs.»

Build yourself a life with a sea view, with a garden. Follow your passions, surround yourself with people who can improve and make you live peacefully and with joy. Also get a dog or a cat if you can; taking care of it will be of great help. Animals can save humans, today more than ever. Avoid everything else, eliminate it from your lives.

Even if for a shorter or longer period you will still be forced into negative situations in which neither growth nor improvement can be breathed, focus on the new environment you are creating and start now to close with the situations that hurt you, and lay the foundations. for others that bring you wellness.

And if it were the last?

Do you remember Rihanna, whom I told you about at the beginning of the chapter? Rihanna did an admirable job on herself over the course of a few weeks. Seriously willing to free herself from the cigarette, she carefully followed the coaching path I proposed to her, becoming to control the stimulus of the cigarette (with the exercise "Thanks, I don't smoke!"), learning to put it off. She answered the questionnaires even if at times, as she is normal, she felt a bit in crisis. On one of these occasions, I suggested that she do this exercise in order to test the progress made:

«Close your eyes and imagine that what you are about to smoke is your last cigarette, you promised yourself. The last cigarette, as if it were a farewell to everything that makes you sick, to all the limiting beliefs about yourself and others, to all the negative situations from which you have not been able to get out so far. The last cigarette, and then you completely change. You smoke this last cigarette with these thoughts in mind. It is not what I would call a pleasant experience, on the contrary, inside you, since you connect it to all this, you hope it will end as soon as possible.

A few more moments and you complete it. Are you there? Now, imagine taking the package and throwing it in the trash. In order to avoid the temptation to retrieve it, you destroy it before throwing it away: you break the cigarettes, you tear the package, you step on it. In short, the package is irrecoverable, it no longer belongs to you. Now open your eyes: how do you feel? ».

«Never been better» Rihanna replied. «A liberation!»

Exercise

Now let's do it together, okay?

1. Imagine smoking your last cigarette. Use all your imagination. Concentrate, turn it on, this is the last time. Visualize the scene in your mind as if it were a movie that flows before your eyes, imagine all the details in a vivid and intense way: the embers that ignite, the sensation of the smoke that falls into your lungs and then you throw out, until consume your last cigarette.

2. Imagine taking the pack with the remaining cigarettes (remember that the last cigarette is a choice, not a constraint because the last one left in the pack or at home) and break it into a thousand pieces, crush it with all the anger you would reserve for who or what has hurt you, has ruined part of your life, for those who said they loved you, but the only thing done is hurt you. Pour on the pack of cigarettes that anger that we often turn against ourselves. Now, the package is destroyed, forever and permanently. Throw away what's left in the garbage can.

3. Now you can breathe deeply and when you visualize yourself in the act of throwing the package forever, repeat aloud "That's enough!" or any other phrase that refers to the decision of freedom.

While doing this, press PIDX.

4. Project your imagination into a moment or situation in your future as a non-smoker, a scene full of wellness and happiness. You are in great shape, surrounded by the people you love. What do you see?

What smells and sounds do you perceive? Are you perhaps at the sea? At a party? Or have you just returned home from work, tired but satisfied? Imagine your favourite situation as if it were a movie, enjoy it fully as you breathe deeply and hold PIDX.

Repeat for 5 times.

If you return to the present with a feeling of relief and the desire to give your best, to take your life back in hand, I congratulate you, you have done a great job! You, like Rihanna, are ready to move on too.

7 ACTION

«I am convinced of the truth of a thought only with a personal commitment».

Ludwig Feuerbach

In society you may seem like strong people, you play an important role, which requires commitment, effort, determination and discipline. You are the best in your profession and even in your family you successfully face a thousand obstacles. You have managed to overcome situations worthy of the worst war. And yet, in front of the cigarette, you become small. How is it possible, if you say, think or show that you are strong? Do you really think you are or do others say so? Either you always are, or you are not. You cannot have great will in work and have no will towards smoking cessation. Will is the excuse for excuses, because it is not quantifiable, it is like hiding behind a finger. Now, it is not necessary to hide, but to admit. Willpower cannot be a justification for smoking for one simple reason: *where we talk about addiction, there is no will*. If you are addicted, there is no *will*.

Addiction goes beyond our will. Those who depend on something or someone would like to get out of it but cannot despite wanting to. Give up this excuse too. First you must empower yourself: develop the intention for wellness, increase your energy, and add a lot of effort. Here is what you need now!

Make your own rules

Dealing with a smoker is not easy at all, you should know that too, right? You will certainly agree with me. Jokes aside, it's not easy. It is important that you give yourself rules. Those necessary to quit and free yourself from cigarettes forever. Now, I will ask you some questions. Answer seriously, take all the time you need because what you write, then you will have to do. At all costs. The most surprising aspect is that it will be up to you to decide what is best for you. However, once you decide, there is no turning back. In the questions I will ask you, you will notice that I speak in the *conditional* and not in the present because I do not assume that you will decide to stop and that you will. It is still all to decide, at least for some, while perhaps others have already decided within themselves. If you were your best, would you choose to free yourself from smoking?

This question helps you to put yourself in the best perspective to make the choice in question. In fact, we often do not realize that we make our choices starting from wrong, uncomfortable and weak positions. This is the fundamental reason why we often make bad decisions. If we were in our best position, we would make wiser decisions, or we would not regret it soon after.

How could you achieve this state of mind? What would you need? What should be checked?

Take your time. You don't have to find the answer instantly, it's normal. You must ask yourself the question several times, look for answers, try hard and maybe even bang your head against the wall until you find the answer you feel is most suitable. Make a commitment to simulate the best state or moods to make your decision. Try to enter it. Evaluate which one might be more effective. Ponder whether with a certain mood you would make a certain choice and whether with another you would take a different one. Think about which one would be most effective for you. You could also decide to take a little of one and a little of the other if you think it could be of benefit to you. Only you know this. It will take some time, but it will be worth it.

_____

_____

_____

If you were now in the optimal state, what would be the date, the day you would choose to free yourself? What do your feelings say?

Decide on the date and the way the choice will happen. Choose a specific day and commit to respecting it. It will be the end of this book, the end of an assignment, the end of the year (I hope you don't take me literally on this aspect unless you are reading me in December), the start of a new job. Specifically, you can link the choice to another event, to a date that is significant for you. Choose freely following the heart.

What would be the first steps you would take? Which is the first? And then? Make a list.

People often forget to act. They think, they wish, they dream, they plan and then they don't act. They drop everything and give up. Instead, you begin by establishing the first step, which is the most important. Then, the second, the third and so on. It is essential. Do it. Take a few days, if you need to, just to answer this question. Because it is about what you will do, the steps that you will put one in front of the other and they are all connected. For example, you could start by creating the right environment within a set time; then continue by changing the power supply; then again throwing the cigarette and finally encouraging others to do the same. You can do whatever you want, however you like. The important thing is that everything is established and put in writing.

In order to evaluate the effectiveness of your answers, measure your feeling of satisfaction. From 1 to 10 how satisfied are you with the answers you have given? What is missing in order to get to 10?

Always keep in mind the answer that you feel most inspiring. It will be your starting point, your base. Also remember that these questions have meaning in the present, in the here and now. In a year everything may be different because you will be different people and therefore your answers will also be different. So avoid answering according to your ideal and trust what you are and what you feel. Be concrete and listen to the heart. The heart is the only one capable of keeping you anchored to your present.

If there is an immortal, it is not you!

"My grandfather smoked 20 cigarettes a day until he was 96 and he never had a cough!"; "My grandfather used to go to the countryside, he still worked like he was 30 years old. He was 85 years old and smoked 30 cigarettes a day!": The smoker's focus is on what supports his "thesis". He sees only what is useful to support his belief. We cannot consciously and voluntarily do something that goes against us, and then we are good enough to invent a system that highlights and confirms our "thesis" and eliminates the interferences that contradict it. How many smokers are there who die of a heart attack at the age of 40? How many at 50? And at 60? How many of tumour? Or emphysema, circulation problems, and a thousand other serious illnesses? When the smoker thinks about the damage of smoke, it is as if, instead of opening a room door to see what is inside, he looks through the keyhole, managing to observe only a limited portion of the space, erasing everything else. Unfortunately, the "rest" exists, especially the damage caused by smoking. Regardless of how many cigarettes you smoke, the danger is real. Now, you can do it: choose, open that door and face the problem.

Do you smoke cigar or pipe?

In the common imagination, smoking a pipe or cigar is an indication of considerable cultural or social stature, a habit of rich industrialists or intellectuals, a status symbol. I could not ask you to stop... you would not be important anymore! Do you understand what it really means? That you need the prosthesis called a cigar or a pipe to play your role, so that others can recognize you as such.

In addition to the terrible stench, be aware that smoking cigars greatly increases the risk of mouth and larynx cancers, because the carbon monoxide (CO) concentrate and the permanence in the mouth are far superior to cigarettes. Just think that an unlit cigar held in the mouth can cause blisters that can become infected. Aspirating cigar smoke causes the highest level of CO poisoning, comparable to that that of those who smoke 60 cigarettes upwards a day. You may be thinking: "But I don't aspire!". I can guarantee you that the perception of smoke aspiration is distorted, not always aware, as happens with the act of breathing. Even if you do not inhale, therefore, you are at risk of intoxication. If you do not believe it, go to any hospital and request a lung co measurement.

How to tell if what you are doing is healthy

Do you like to play sports? Is there something you are good at? Let's say you enjoy playing basketball. What would your goal be? Making more baskets than the opponent, right? Imagine taking part in a basketball game in which all the free throws you manage to make in a set amount of time, say 15 minutes, are counted. Let's assume the world record is 300 baskets. And you make 320. Now, you are the champions. What do you do? You feel proud of the victory, you tell it around, you want to teach others your skills, to pass on the values, beliefs and growth that come with it, right? Good!

Now I would like you to explain to me why the opposite happens with cigarettes. We said that the better you are, the more positive it is, the prouder you are, and you teach it to others, correct? We do the exact opposite with smoke. You are proud if you take a few "hits", if you smoke less. If, on the other hand, you take a lot of shots, you feel ashamed of yourself and do not tell it around. You do not want others to learn about "smoking" from you, especially your loved ones.

There is only one explanation for all this: smoking is "bad", and you do not want others to emulate you. When you do not want to be an example to others, when you tend to hide, it means that what you are doing is "harmful". Just as you care that your children, grandchildren, partners learn from you what you are good at and that can help them grow. This is healthy.

You are an example for someone

Just being there makes you an example for someone. Words often have no effect on others, who instead mimic your way of being, especially children. If you are a doctor, patients imitate you; as well as your nephews, if you are involving uncles or aunts, whom they love; athletes if you are a coach, or a champion. Adults smoke, often without realizing, offer a negative example to young people, who tend to imitate significant figures such as family members they highly esteem and intimately hope to be like one day. There are important and famous people who are admired and even emulated by young people among smokers. "I can't think of everyone!", You are thinking right now. Instead, you must do it. Because as adults we have a responsibility to pass on the best to future generations. If you have a role in society, you need to respect it and do your best. I do not want to teach you how to behave, I just want to make you think.

From a research carried out between 1998 and 2005 by the Department of Addictions at ass3 Alto Friuli[23], it emerged that in young people the habit of

---

[23] G. Canzian, "Fumo e adolescenti nell'Alto Friuli. Evoluzione dei consumi (1998-2005) e correlazione con altri comportamenti di abuso", «Tabaccologia», 2007, 1, pp. 25-31.

smoking, as well as alcohol abuse, is closely related to the habits of parents. Therefore, despite the advice that you can provide in words alone, it is very likely that your son, your daughter and anyone else who takes an example from you, imitates what you yourself do. In these cases, the "Don't do what I do" rule does not apply. The clear and direct message that arrives is: "What I do is right. You can do it too!". The same study shows that smoking leads the way to other addictions. In fact, alcohol abuse is present only in 3% of subjects who had never smoked, while for smokers, alcohol abuse rises to 40% of the subjects interviewed. The same mechanism for all other drugs, legal and illegal, from coffee, to cannabis, to heroin: from 3% of use for non-smokers to 73% for smokers. Because despite what a person might think, I have already said, it is not the joint that opens the doors to other drugs and addictions: it is the cigarette. In other words, smoking exemplifies how to create strong addictions. You can avoid this by focusing on your own wellness. What you do must bring well-being to you and to the people influenced by your behaviour. There is always someone who takes you as an example. Eliminate harmful habits and create new empowering habits. Then, for the next 30 days, dedicate yourself to an empowering activity - which you may already be doing - and try to involve others, encourage them to fall in love with your own healthy passion. Develop the habit of reading, sports, healthy eating and infect everyone who is close to you. You will notice the big difference from before, you will get rewarding results, and the people you care about you will be grateful to you. Adopt someone, educate them to improvement through what you are experienced with. In addition to saving yourself, you can save those you love by your example.

The right moment

How many times have I heard it! "This is not the right time!", "In this period I am too busy and stressed, it is not the right time", "I need to fix my problems before I quit, it is not the right time", etc. There are many smokers to whom I have heard: "At the moment I am too stressed from work, as soon as I go on vacation, I will stop smoking!". During the holiday period, then, they postponed further because they wanted to enjoy relaxation without commitments. There are hundreds of other excuses I could have included. I will spare you; you know more than me. But know that when you do not decide, someone else does it for you: the cigarette! Whenever you postpone and repeat in your head "This is not the right time", it is the cigarette that controls you and decides for you! This reinforces the

---

http://www.tabaccologia.it/PDF/1_2007/6_12007.pdf 26 "I figli di fumatori calcheranno le orme dei genitori", «La Stampa», 08/08/2013. http://www.lastampa.it/2013/08/08/societa/mamme/salute/i-figli-di-fumatori-calcheranno-le-orme-dei-genitori-zCB4mSdbLuQvpgP128xTFJ/pagina.html

addiction. The more you postpone, the weaker you become. Taking a sample of 500 people I had in counselling, I could see that it is more *effective* to get rid of cigarettes in a difficult moment. Mainly because:

1. The principle of urgency is activated, since quitting smoking becomes an integral part of a wider difficulty and at the same time of the solution. A tie is created between the "difficult moment" and the search for new solutions which constitutes a very important push. In other words, under stress, people are led to change their automatic response, looking for new wellness strategies.

2. Motivation increases. When you associate smoking deconditioning with an improvement in your life, the two aspects bind and reinforce each other. For example, if you want to free yourself from cigarettes and, at the same time, reach an ideal physical shape, you have two goals on your side that motivate and support each other, amplifying wellness. Creating such a link is important, despite those who think that doing multiple things together can be an overload. In fact, sometimes you will perceive greater improvements on one side only, others you will notice them on both; either way, you will always have that feeling of growth that will keep you motivated. This increases your chances of success and reduces the chances of relapse compared to those who say they wait for the "moment of peace" to break free from smoking.

3. You become more aware. The "difficult moment", in fact, is symptomatic of a disease with consequent negative repercussions on work, couple life, friendships, one's own wellness. People who manage to quit smoking in this moment are those who choose to stop making fun of themselves and take responsibility for blaming the outside world for their malaise and understand instead that the results depend on the choices "made" as well as those "not done". In virtue of this, they decide to eliminate what pollutes their life and create new relationships with what feeds wellness at 360 degrees. The cigarette falls fully into the category of malaise.

The pseudo-decision to quit in the moment of serenity predisposes to relapse. The occurrence of a difficulty, a stressful situation, a discomfort, an event that weighs on the psycho-physical conditions of the person can reactivate the "smoking mechanism". The best way to react is to defuse the automatic reaction to the cigarette in moments of crisis, replacing it with a response oriented towards wellness.

A question of balance

The difficulty is nothing more than a manifest opportunity for change: in a condition of apparent equilibrium, the external environment forces the person's inner environment, which most of the time reacts by opposing this pressure. Many people think, hope and try daily not to change anything in their life, which they know well by now. The difficulty of human change lies in not knowing what is to come; many tend to remain in the condition in which they find themselves for fear of the unknown.

Try to think about when you walk. Unless you are drunk, you feel balanced when you move. Do you know why? Walking is now automatic, natural and spontaneous for you. The sensation of perennial balance is a game between the momentary imbalance of standing on one foot and the next step that gives stability, and so on. We are so used to walking that we no longer pay attention to the possibility of falling, we feel that we are always in balance, but this is not the case. Ultimately, equilibrium is that condition in which we already know what will happen, what the next step will be, but it is not static, it is movement.

The same happens in the life of each of us. There is no person in the world who can remain immobile in a psychological, emotional and therefore relational condition. We change, that's how we are. Serenity must be created in the movement of life, not rejecting change. The only way you can get rid of cigarettes (addictions) is to do it on the go, not in an "easy", static, pseudo-serenity moment. Such a moment basically does not exist in anyone's life. We are in constant motion. Find your balance as you walk, naturally. Once you know you can do it, it's forever. Now, move and walk towards your wellness despite everything.

The cell and habit

Imagine that habit is a cell. We know that man is an animal of habit. He follows patterns that he knows and thanks to which he faces everyday life. He could not make it up all over again every day. Are you there? This cell has an important function for the body, it helps it survive. Sometimes cells are altered in their DNA by external agents; their function is no longer the same, from that moment on the other cells that are born contain the new modified DNA and reproduce by massing, taking away space for healthy cells and here we are in front of a cancer. It works like this. What is the external agent that in the case of the smoker modifies the DNA of the healthy habit, turning it into a cancerous habit? The thought, first oriented towards one's own well-being and then towards disease. The smoker's thinking is such as to transform the healthy cell oriented to wellness (the healthy habit) into a cancer cell oriented to malaise (the habit of smoking), which becomes metastasis in the situation of overt addiction. The most important aspect to understand is that by reorienting your thoughts towards wellness, you can heal your cells and strengthen them.

However, it is important to underline that if the habits in place are not recognized, it is not possible to change them. Addiction to cigarettes is a harmful habit. However, addiction does not arise from the act of smoking itself, from behaviour, but from what drives the smoker to take a cigarette: the stimulus and expectation. The two most important aspects of the vicious circle are these. The stimulus is what activates the behaviour, the expectation is what you think you will achieve after repeating the gesture. Now, I have a task for you. Over the course of the next week, you will need to make a note on a piece of paper, as you feel it, what kind of stimulus it is. What's the spark? A situation, a thought, a state of mind? An emotion, a feeling? Finally, describe what you expected by smoking. What would be the satisfaction? What would you have earned? What empowering and wellness behaviour could you attach to the same stimulus, which gives you the same expectation, the same result?

1. Identify the type of stimulus.

2. Find out the expectation.

3. Identify a substitute behaviour that gratifies the expectation and is proactive, empowering and improving.

David, after performing this task for a week, noticed that he felt more the stimulus of the cigarette during work breaks. In those moments he hoped that his shift would end soon because he had the desire to smoke. So the expectation combined to the cigarette was the feeling that the working day would end quickly. Having identified this mechanism, David decided to introduce a new behaviour, different from the cigarette, which pushed him to be more productive, in order to feel that time was passing quickly. So whenever he felt the urge to smoke, he tidied up his room - even for a few minutes. Margaret, on the other hand, smoked more when she found herself involved in stressful personal situations, at work or in private life. Reflecting, she understood that this was the stimulus which pushed her to light another cigarette and that, when she warned it, she expected the person she was discussing with at that moment to stop talking. She had a personal difficulty dealing with disputes with those she was attached to. She felt invaded. In particular, the moments of "smoking" behaviour's activation were two: the moments of meeting / confrontation with the boss at work, and the moments of discussion with the family in private life.

She realized that in these two situations the vicious circle inevitably started. She could not control it, when it happened, she even did not realize it. She was one of those smokers who had a cigarette still lit in the ashtray and automatically lit another one, such was the pressure she suffered. During and after the cigarette she experienced a feeling of "power" that she did not have at other times. It was the only moment in which she was the one to decide and not to suffer as it often happened. What did she do? Whenever she felt the urge, she got into the habit of blocking the ongoing discussion by asking her interlocutor the courtesy to use another tone, to be more understanding without harassing her too much.

Therefore, she began to put the right distance in order not to feel invaded and to be respected. She learned to communicate better with herself and with others: starting to listen to herself, in order to declare her feelings and thoughts, leading the other towards a better understanding and communication. Ferdinand noticed that he lit more cigarettes when he felt oppressed, when he felt a sense of imprisonment. He did not like his job, he did it out of a sense of duty and that is it. However, this situation caused him a strong discomfort. When the feeling of oppression, almost anguish, became stronger, then the investigated behaviour would take off: Ferdinando looked for the package in his pocket and smoked. The feeling he got from smoking, he told me, was one of freedom, excitement and power. His gratification was to experience that longed-for and distant feeling of freedom. It was the only way to be able to reach it, as he thought. He had not understood that this was the reason that pushed him to smoke and that made him indispensable until that moment. Finally, he went looking for another job that satisfied him and changed his life. You understand well that each of them began to think differently. After becoming aware of the smoking mechanism, they implemented new actions which then resulted in a significant change in their life. They went to discover the unknown that awaited them.

Get out of your Comfort Zone

Many people seem confused when you talk about wellness. They tell me they know what's good for them, but then they do quite the opposite. This dystonia generates great frustration and anger. I do not know about you, in my opinion, it was like this every time I tricked wellness without ever reaching it. If I know what's good for me, why not go get it now?

Now smile, take a deep breath and look differently at your life, friends, relationships, yourself; feel that your energy has changed, it is stronger. Wellness is often outside the commonly shared and practiced thinking patterns. The human tendency is to remain in the known patterns and therefore not to change except within these limits, which also have a containment function. This zone is called by change experts the "Comfort Zone". The Comfort Zone is not a sign of well-being, nor of malaise; it is simply the set of a person's habits: thoughts, feelings, actions and results. It is what is known, which is why people repeat the same pattern repeatedly until they understand that, in order to improve, they must change it again. The smoker is trapped in his own Comfort Zone. Why? Because he thinks of getting out of what he knows feels discomfort and fear. Maybe he tries or has tried in the past and then came back. But now things are different, now you know that you must necessarily be uncomfortable for some time and cross the Discomfort Zone to get out of your Comfort Zone. There is nothing to be afraid of, the feeling of discomfort only means that you are leaving your Comfort Zone, the haven, to go towards new discoveries. You can do it by committing yourself to learn new and healthy habits. Remember that discomfort will push you to retrace your steps: this is where you will have to make a difference, training daily. After just 30 days of training following the advice contained in the book, the new Zone will become your Comfort one, where you will be comfortable with yourself and with others without resorting to cigarettes. Know that this area is always in motion and you will have to change it again, always. This is true for everyone, no one can escape change. If you accept this fact and open yourself to change, you will always live in a state of wellness.

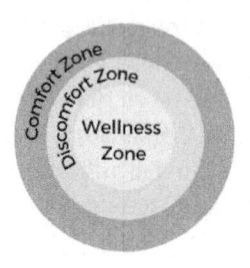

Today I ask you to act for yourself, for your life and for those around you. I suggest that you contextualize the change and plan it in a preparatory way, starting from your current state to reach the ideal one. By "context" I mean your age, your economic, sentimental situation, your daily commitments, your job, in short, the various areas of your life. Make a map of who you are and what you have in relation to the goal to be achieved.

For example, if you are not satisfied with your physical fitness, think about the ideal you want and evaluate how to achieve it starting from the current situation, or rather, considering your age, weight, your state of health, the time you have available for devote yourself to sports, etc. Why all this? Because everything contributes to achieve the result. If only one of these conditions is not taken into consideration, you could miss the goal and be disheartened. A person older in age, for example, could choose to take longer walks and take care of their diet. This may be enough for her to achieve her goal. This is what I mean by contextualizing: you must customize. A young person who wants to improve could instead go for a run, join the gym, participate in competitions and tournaments, play team sports and take care of nutrition, etc. Choose based on your individual characteristics and availability. By sifting through all the features, you will better manage your time by organizing it according to the goals you have set for yourself: for example, if you work all day without any opportunity in the evening, you might consider getting up an hour earlier in the morning to play sports.

When your starting state is clear, you will be able to organize yourself better for the purposes of your ideal. Set yourself mini-goals, milestones, and choose a path that you find fun. Launch yourself towards the goal with enthusiasm. Do what you like and make you feel good, look for new stimuli to support your ideal.

Go through the Discomfort Zone

Remember that there may be resistance to change. Even if you think you want to achieve something, the fact of taking a new path, leaving the reassuring old routines, after all, could scare you. Therefore a blockage could arise, self-sabotage mechanisms could take over.

It is precisely for this reason that I suggest you dedicate yourself to something that is a source of pleasure, fun, gratification for you, because only these moments will be able to mitigate the feeling of discomfort. For example, if you are a woman who always and only thinks about family, husband, children, mother-in-law, friends, in short, if you are obsessed with the idea of the "perfect mother" and you never have a moment for yourself, the only one the thought of dedicating time to it could generate "feelings of guilt" in you. Your Comfort Zone encompasses everything you do to take care of your family at all costs, to the detriment of yourself. So, you understand well how the Comfort Zone is not necessarily an area where you feel good; it is an area that is preferred only because it is known while what is not known is restless.

A woman who believes she neglects others if she thinks about herself, probably learned as a child that dedicating him to himself is selfish, and that one is "good" only if one dedicates body and soul to others, who as a "commodity exchange" return love. If you live by this thought pattern, going through the zone of discomfort will mean for you to start thinking about yourself dealing with guilt and running the "risk" of not receiving love (at least according to your old thought pattern). Is that clear to you? The wellness area is a step further, where you feel good about yourself without a cigarette, you are happy and, for this reason, you support and help others better too, free from the guilt feelings that you will discover are of no use.

Exercise

You are growing increasingly more. The cigarette is getting even smaller; now, visualize it in front of you as it shrinks at the speed of light, so small you can crush it. Imagine doing it now. As you step on the cigarette, the feeling of freedom pervades you. You cannot avoid it. If something inside is opposed, you are a hundred times stronger. The cigarette is there, small, squashed, abandoned forever. And as you press the index finger and thumb of your right hand (PIDX) together, relive the scene in your mind with ever more vivid images, sounds and your inner dialogue. Pay attention to the negative sensations that fade until they disappear to make room for pure energy and inner strength. Repeat 5 times.

Imagine your "wellness oasis"

Whenever you feel discomfort, it will also be motivating to realize that you are inevitably in the Intermediate Zone and, in order to remember that one step a day, you are approaching the goal of wellness. With this awareness in mind, move on. Imagine yourself in this increasingly difficult journey as you step out of your Comfort Zone and feel arousal; smile and visualize in front of you the oasis of wellness, which you will discover to be your new place, your new Comfort Zone. Imagine that you are already there and describe how you feel. What do you see around you? What sounds, voices and noises do you hear? Close your eyes to enter the scene and focus on the sensations it arouses in you.

Best describe your new Comfort Zone:

_____

_____

_____

In order to be free from any kind of addiction you need an inner balance that only we can create. If the balance is generated by something or someone external to us, it is a "false" balance. We are the fulcrum of our wellness in relation to the outside world. If we find ourselves in a condition of inner imbalance, we are prone to establish unbalanced relationships, such as the bond with the cigarette. If we are in balance, we will create balanced relationships. Choose to improve your life far beyond just quitting smoking. It will all become much more powerful. Make quitting smoking a decisive step in achieving a goal that is very important to you, such as achieving optimal physical fitness for example. Quit smoking and paint your house. Buy a more beautiful one. Quit smoking and change that job that's too tight on you. Quit smoking and start training for a competition. Connect the changes and the result will create a much more powerful effect.

5 key concepts to keep in mind

As you free yourself, you become more and more a non-smoker:

1. Accept the state you are in with the desire in your heart to evolve and free yourself. Commit yourself not 50% but 100%, with every part of you.

2. The principle of urgency! Do you know it? It is that drive that makes you realize the results. We often practice it throughout our lives, but mostly badly. Now use it for yourself and for your wellness. If you do not do it now, you may not have the opportunity anymore.

Imagine what you will be like by continuing to smoke. Imagine reaching a state of severe discomfort and imagine that you can only avoid it if you stop now. You run out of time.

Mark on the line from 1 to 10 how much this thought creates you the urge to quit smoking now.

1								10

Well, now you think that in ten years you will die from smoking, in very bad conditions, attached to an oxygen cylinder.

Mark on the line from 1 to 10 how much this thought creates you the urge to quit smoking now.

1									10

Now you think you will die within 3 months if you do not stop now.

Mark on the line 1 to 10 how much this thought creates you the urge to quit smoking now.

1									10

You think it will happen exactly in 30 days if you do not stop now and forever.

Mark on the line 1 to 10 how much this thought creates you the urge to quit smoking now.

1									10

This is the principle of urgency! This principle is useful when there is indeed time left to commit to changing things. When there is nothing left to do, however, it creates frustration, pain and discomfort. You can do it but, you still have time. Right now!

1. **Commitment.** How long are you willing to put in? Declare publicly your intention and the commitment you are making. Meet the "fear of failure", knowing that if you are tempted to retrace your steps, you will be judged for not having made it. Remember that failure does not exist, and that it is just another way to learn how to get results. You have no more excuses!

2. **Discipline.** Practice everything you find here.

Do the exercises every day and repeat the mantras. All time. Do it, at least, for the duration of the book's reading. Everyday. Try not to pass a day without doing the exercises. Even if you do not want to, just do it. Discipline is the antidote to renunciation.

3. Persevere. Any difficulty you may have in following the suggestions is just a matter of desire, will, goals and commitment.

Improvement is change

Getting rid of the cigarette is improving, therefore changing. Change comes from within; sometimes it is slow, sometimes fast, it depends on your state. Everyone is different, don't you agree?

Everyone can achieve a radical change; the difference is in training. Great champions do not differ from others in talent; they stand out for their commitment, dedication, determination, discipline and daily training. The goal is clear. In moments of great pain, when you think you cannot do it, you cannot, that desire for revenge, that anger that turns into energy, that desire to reach the goal that becomes stronger despite everything, is triggered. Not a day goes by without a true champion not training, even with his mind. Similarly, you have learned to be a smoker. At the beginning you did not have any talent, instead look at yourself now: you are cigarette professionals. Did you start with 30 cigarettes a day? Of course not! You started gradually and in the space of a few years you came to smoke the number of cigarettes you smoke today. Getting rid of the cigarette is a path of improvement that involves:

1. the mind (the system of thoughts).

2. the body (sensations, emotions, physical wellness).

3. actions (empowering behaviours, language).

In the paragraphs below, we will delve into each of these areas. We will reflect together on how to train and strengthen them for a 360 ° well-being.

Experience

I don't know if you usually learn from your mistakes. If you did, you probably would not smoke today. What do I mean? If you have been smoking for several years it means that you are not learning from your mistakes, at least about the cigarette. Each cigarette smoked is a mistake, but also a learning. If you see it only as a mistake it is not useful for your wellness, while it is if you consider it as a learning process. Any failed attempt is not a failure, it is a learning process. The mistakes of those who have died because of the cigarette are a learning for those who are alive. The knowledge we have about the harm of smoking is learning. Nicotine withdrawal is learning. All we do is learning. Our life is learning.

Have you ever wondered why there are people who always make the same mistakes? Those who go in and out of prison or who always find the wrong partners or who always launch into bankrupt business ventures. Why do none of them change their patterns even though he has good reasons to do so? Bad luck? No. They simply do not admit that they have made a mistake, they do not accept "failure" and, therefore, cannot turn it into teaching. These people rather tend to erase it. They do not experience it first hand, but as if it happened to others. They distance themselves emotionally from it. Admitting failure is painful. Most people prefer to avoid pain by emotionally distancing themselves from the event, blaming others. Instead, recognizing failure, physically feeling the pain caused by bad choices imprints a message in our emotional memory that, subsequently, will be useful for new learning. After I accept failure, I can ask myself: "What has this situation taught me?", "How can I use this new knowledge for my growth?" These are life-saving questions that bring you closer to the result, that change your perspective. If this process is not experienced, learning is not possible and despite having had direct experience of something dare, you will not be able to turn it to your advantage. Direct experience is the first and greatest source of learning we have.

There are no mistakes, there is learning!

Another way to learn, very neglected but effective, is indirect experience, or rather, learning by reworking the others' experience. According to this principle, the experience could also come from other sources: a story heard, a newspaper article, a book read, etc. they can have a great emotional impact, such as to leave their imprint in our memory and subsequently be used as learning. People who also learn from the others' experiences live them as in first person, putting themselves in those persons' shoes and being able to draw a lesson from their stories. They can mentally move over time to learn from past events and think about the implications of their situation in the future, applying the lessons learned and experiencing the situations to come. I sincerely suggest that you learn from past mistakes. Be your own judges, but not the executioners. Use your learning to save them. Learn from other smokers, from the lessons explained in this book, from newspaper articles, from short stories. Amplify them and experience them first hand. Take a story and relive it as if it were your own, try to feel like the protagonists. Do it and it will really be like that. Avoiding identification, maintaining the gap, is not an advantage, it is not very intelligent. On the contrary, living and amplifying situations makes the difference between feeling good or bad today as well as tomorrow; between learning and not learning. It is giving the right meaning to things. If you learn from experience, everything becomes a result, it turns into feedback. Failure turns into learning.

Cigarette and body weight

Studies[24] have shown that the smoker lives in a condition of artificial thinness, about 3.5 kg below their actual weight. It means that an 80kg smoker would weigh 83.5kg if he did not smoke. "How much would you weigh without the smoke? What a crap, yuck! Too fat! And who looks at you more! My God, what a horrible thing! If you have this difficulty you absolutely must not quit smoking... you don't want to get fat!"

According to the same studies, in the first three months of cessation about 3 kg are assimilated due to the metabolism, previously altered by the cigarette, changes again, in the sense that it slows down. In this transitional period you risk gaining a few pounds while maintaining the same diet. After the third month, the metabolism normalizes and returns to work as before the cigarette. Take advantage of this moment to start a correct and healthy diet or in any case adopt new diets, do what is necessary to stay healthy and keep fit. By quitting smoking, in addition to being cigarette free, you will be free to decide on your weight and shape without the conditioning of the cigarette. Quitting smoking means losing weight in a natural, functional and effective way, and keeping really fit. The first real advantage is the metabolic rebalancing; the second is the increase in self-esteem thanks to evident results. By quitting smoking you will feel better and healthier, you will love yourself more and you will do more things to keep yourself fit, such as an intelligent and pleasant diet, oriented to wellness. At the same time, eating healthily will make you feel even better about yourself. All former smokers associate cessation with a feeling of wellness.

They feel better and have higher self-esteem. Decide to quit smoking and, at the same time, adopt a healthy diet: you will lose weight and purify yourself more quickly. You will be more motivated because the benefits will be multiple, but the

---

[24] M. Truncellito, "Stop al fumo senza ingrassare", http://www.truncellito.com/1999/smettere-di-fumare-senza-ingrassare

effort will be concentrated in the same time frame. Doing both things together requires the same commitment of one thing, the focus is even more concentrated, and the results come sooner because they support each other. Losing one pound will motivate you to continue to do without cigarettes and continue exercising. Not smoking for 10 days will encourage you to follow a healthier diet and maybe start exercising. Put these elements together and the result will be extraordinary. Choose to practice a sport that is competitive, that puts you in a position to exceed your limits. Set yourself goals, overcome yourself, commit yourself, improve and sweat. Pushing your limits pushes toxic thoughts out of your mind and generates new energy, just as sweating helps eliminate toxins from the body. Compete with yourself and then also with others. Make a list of activities that promote well-being and that can make your life better (es: getting rid of cigarettes, eating a healthy diet, etc.). Enter sport, hobbies and all that can be useful to you:

_____

_____

_____

I will never be tired of repeating that the cigarette is a way to disguise a discomfort that the person is unable to face and resolve. So aiming at behaviour alone, taking out the cigarette does not help much; this explains the reason for the failure of many smokers. Make a commitment to feel good in all areas of your life, and you will be successful.

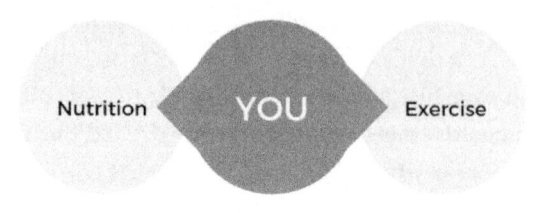

Creating harmony and balance in all areas of life generates wellness, mental, emotional and relational stability.

Time travel

What signal triggers the idea of smoking in you? What makes you want to take and smoke a cigarette?

Exercise

Imagine having to explain to a person the process that occurs when you smoke, starting from your thoughts. What comes to your mind? Do you see an image of you lighting a cigarette and the stimulus is triggered? Do you hear a voice inside telling you "It's time to smoke?" What is the first thought that triggers the stimulus?

Write it here:

Now, take this image and add the sounds and sensations it gives you. If it is a voice, add images and sensations. Make sure you are inside the scene, experience it as if you were there. Now, press the thumb and index finger of the left hand together (PISX). Very good! If you are doing the exercise correctly, you should try the stimulus of the cigarette. If you are not, let it comes. Reinforce the image, retrace the scene like in a movie. Associate, or rather, enter the scene and experience it. Listen to the sounds and voices, focus on the sensations. Okay! Take all these images, make them smaller, put them in the lower left corner as if on a screen, move them away from you until they become a dot. Hold it there.

Now imagine your desired state, what and how you would like to be without the cigarette. Imagine yourself as on a screen distant from you. Keep the vivid image in front of you, without going into it: you must remain dissociated from it. Observe yourself as you have already reached your ideal state, notice what you are like after you are liberated. What do you do to the best of your potential? How do you move, what posture do you have? What sounds are there? What voices do you hear? How do you speak? Is your tone the same as before or is it different? What sensations does it give you to see the film of your ideal state? Intensely and vividly represent the film of how you will be, complete with sounds and sensations. Approach the screen, large in front of you, without going into it. The feeling you should feel, doing the exercise well, is one of greater desire. You should feel increasingly more willing to go in and enjoy the scene. The closer the screen is, the more the sensation grows. Make this screen even bigger, improve its brightness, sounds and sensations. Now, if you feel a great attraction to enter the image, you are there! Press the thumb and index finger of the right hand together (PIDX).

Repeat this exercise at least 5 times to anchor it well.

Your ecological ideal

Before moving on, let's try to understand if this desired state you want to achieve, which you are already close to, is ecological. What do I mean by ecological? According to your whole being. If you are not, you should review it. In order to understand all this better, answer these questions: Have you contextualized yourself, free from the cigarette, in the real world? Have you imagined yourself in real, everyday situations and conditions? What do you see?

_____

_____

_____

Let's try to go into details together. Imagine that you are finally and free from the cigarette. What are the qualities / skills / abilities you have in your new condition (how do you feel - how do you walk - what tone of voice do you use - how is your body - how do you relate to others - with your partner - etc.)? You must be clear about the qualities of the new you, non-smoker.

_____

Dwell on your ideal non-smoking status (you can help yourself tracing the image by squeezing your thumb and index finger of your right hand), visualize it as if on a screen placed a couple of steps away from you. What do you have to do to be able to enter? What steps do you need to take? What kind of commitment do you need to do?

Imagine the scene, the screen is in front of you, the sensations it transmits to you are getting stronger and you would like to enter it, but you still cannot do it. What do you have to do to have the right to take one step closer to the scene, then another one step closer to entering it? Imagine taking the first step, visualize yourself as you are about to do it, write down what behaviour it corresponds to (it could be re-reading this book, applying one of the suggestions, doing an exercise or something else). Question the deepest part of you, clear your mind and ask yourself: what is the first step to be a non-smoker? Be careful! This is a delicate and important moment, take a deep breath as you go inside yourself to question the deepest part of you and repeat the question: "What is the first step to be a non-smoker?"

This is the first thing you will do! Congratulations, that's fine! Now, imagine that you have done this, having taken the first step. Take a much deeper breath to go even lower and ask your deeper part, "What is the second step to be a non-smoker?"

This is the second thing you will do and so on until you get to the last step, before entering the screen and experiencing the desired situation. At the last step, ask yourself what you need to do to permanently and forever access your ideal area, to be and live as your ideal, non-smoker self. Write it down. Write down what you will do for this crucial passage into the new zone, from which you will never go back. From today you will always look forward, towards your wellness. Now, ask yourself: "What can I and should I do to take my last step and become a non-smoker?"

_____

_____

_____

Once you reach the desired state, what will you lose? (there are usually inner and unaware conflicts. Sometimes reaching one result means losing another, and this creates a fight. This is the cause of many failures, including not being able to quit smoking. Behind such failure could be. hiding the fear of not having arguments in common during a chat between friends or acquaintances, or the fear of having difficulty in approaching a potential partner in a club, or the fear of gaining weight, as we have seen before). The cigarette guarantees a certain result. What could you lose without the cigarette?

_____

_____

_____

Now you know what and how you will do it.

Exercise

Let's go back to the previous year. Think of the cigarette, the image or the associated "video", the sounds and sensations that make you feel the stimulus. Press the index finger and thumb of your left hand (PISX) together. Amplify the scene, join in, you are in, live it. Shrink it and quickly move it away, until it becomes a dot, and place it at the bottom left as if on a screen in front of you. The screen is blank now. You do not feel the same sensations as before, are you aware of it? Do you see what power your mind has?

Now, visualize the image of the desired state together with the sounds and feelings that accompany it, retrieve the entire scene and observe it as if it were placed on the usual screen. Zoom in on the scene, amplify the sounds and concentrate on the sensations, on how they grow gradually. Approach the scene without entering it yet and feel how the desire to be part of it increases and become yourself, free from the cigarette. Increase the brightness and sounds like on a high-fidelity screen, focus on the sensations that go through your body. Press the index finger and thumb of your right hand together (PIDX). Very good. Repeat the exercise 5 times as a strengthening. Each time you repeat the scene of your ideal state (as a non-smoking), do this: first shrink it, move it away until it becomes a dot on the right of the screen, then snap the image from dot to full screen. Repeat for 5 times. Shrink and zoom in. Good. Now, let's complete the exercise to see its effectiveness. Make everything smaller. Done? The screen is free. Click the dot on the left and associate with the negative image in which you smoke, recover all the sensations connected to it. At the same time you zoom out this image and move it away from you, zoom in on the right image to full screen, associate a sound or sentence with your voice (for example: "Good job!"), while held down together index and thumb of the right hand (PIDX).

Let's recap:

1. A Negative image associated.

2. As soon as you reduce the negative image on the left, the positive one from the right automatically expands across the entire screen.

3. While repeating the sentence or sound chosen, press and hold the index finger and thumb of your right hand (PIDX) together.

4. Repeat the exercise 5 times, even faster.

This part could be challenging because you are not used to it. But tomorrow it will be easier and day after day the feelings of wellness will be increasingly more spontaneous. Remember that the more you repeat the exercise, the more you will change the neurological structure connected to the cigarette, or rather you will create a new one linked to your wellness, while the one connected to the cigarette will atrophy until it disappears. Maybe in part it has already happened. Do you know when the direction of a street's travel is changed in the city? It will have happened to everyone sometimes to take the road travelled daily for years, and suddenly notice something wrong: a car in the opposite sense towards you. "But people are crazy!" You exclaim. Then, there is the doubt: maybe they have changed direction? You realize that you are in contradiction. So, what do you do?

Back off, apologize, thank those who kindly showed you the right path, and move on. The next day, taken by your thoughts, approaching the usual road, what are you doing? Slow down as if you want to take it, suddenly remember, someone behind you is ringing to warn you, apologize and continue. The scene repeats itself for at least a week, because by now an automatism had been created. In the meantime, you have a way to learn a new route to get to your destination. Now you can go the usual way in reverse. After a month, your new habit is to get off that road. You no longer remember that before, you could only enter there, right? For you now, this is the new path, the new meaning. As well as being a non-smoker.

"Electronic cigarette" and nicotine substitutes

Initially I thought that the electronic cigarette (but the correct term would be "vaporizer") was useless. I thought either "smoke" or "quit"!

Then, noticing the spread of the phenomenon, I began to reflect on it and talk about it with smokers. So I understood: my judgment had been too hasty. The interest in the electronic cigarette is proof that everyone wants to get rid of cigarettes: from the smell and the daily lace. All smokers want to get better. The e-cigarette phenomenon must be valued and not suppressed as some try to do. If a smoker buys an electronic cigarette, this gesture can be understood as a first step towards awareness; in fact, it is as if he is publicly admitting that he wants to get rid of tobacco. In fact, it is easy to understand that those who are willing to put themselves in a ridiculous condition in the others' eyes - taking that kind of "electronic pacifier" with them - really want to get rid of the cigarette.

Personally, I believe that the negative news reported in magazines, newspapers and online articles against vaporizers is aimed at discrediting their use. I am not saying that the electronic cigarette is good for you and that it is a source of pride to keep it around your neck or in your hand all day to "suck it", and it is also true that it is not a natural product, but it is still the most valid alternative after total cessation from smoking. An Italian study led by Professor Mangiaracina has already shown in 2012 that the electronic cigarette is much less harmful than tobacco and is not carcinogenic, although it is not completely harmless, but the same professor, in an interview given to me while I was writing this book, explained that, in terms of damage, it would be like comparing "a dinghy to an ocean liner".25 Therefore, it is not excluded that the interests of the tobacco multinationals are behind the electronic cigarette's demonization. Each of us should learn to filter communication, to understand better in order to choose more consciously. Scientific data can be published by highlighting some characteristics rather than others; the information can be manipulated. I will give you an example: there are studies that confirm the increase in the threshold of attention in smokers thanks to nicotine. Of course, it is an exciting substance! But, if a newspaper publishes an article entitled "The cigarette improves attention", as I read years ago, it is manipulating information, as it is generalizing without specifying the context of the study, deleting some negative information and thus distorting the meaning.

The business of smoking

Let's go back to the "electronic cigarette" just for a moment. On the one hand, there are those who argue that "electronic cigarettes" are harmful; on the other, the consequences on the health of traditional cigarettes are undeniable, just as it cannot be denied that their sale, worldwide, constitutes a tour of 'business of several billion (a good 147.4 according to some estimates).26

---

25 G. Mangiaracina et al., «Electronic cigarettes: an evaluation of exposure to chemicals and fine particulate matter (pm)», Ann Ig. 2012, Jul-Aug; 24 (4), pp. 279-88.
https://www.ncbi.nlm.nih.gov/pubmed/22913171

26 A. Franceschi, "Quanto vale il mercato della sigaretta? Tutti i numeri di un business che fa milioni di morti e miliardi di utili", «Il Sole 24 Ore», 03/02/2014. http://www. ilsole24ore.com/art/notizie/2013-11-06/quanto-vale-mercato-sigaretta-tutti-numeri-un-business-che-fa-milioni-morti-e-miliardi-utili-163805.shtml?uuid=ABZOTvb

Let us reflect on what would happen if "electronic cigarettes" were to establish themselves on the market. These are some of the considerations that came to my mind following a series of research and that I would like to share with you:

- the tobacco multinationals would record a reduction in turnover in the order of hundreds of millions of euros.

- the pharmaceutical multinationals would record a decrease in the sale of nicotine substitutes. A further difficulty for pharmaceutical companies would be the decline in the sales of drugs to treat people affected by smoking. You did not think about this, did you? It would mean having a significant drop in cancers, heart attacks, pulmonary emphysema and many other smoking-related diseases. The economic damage from not "selling" these drugs would be majestic for these companies.

- On the contrary, the State, despite selling cigarettes, would have a huge profit if people quit smoking or preferred the "electronic cigarette". I do not intend to advertise the "electronic cigarette" because, for the reasons I have told you about, I am in favour of totally natural methods, but - I repeat - it is certainly preferable to the traditional cigarette. In Italy, health expenditure to treat sick people suffering from smoking-related diseases has enormous costs: it is around 6 billion euros. Not to mention the fact that in our country about 90,000 deaths per year are attributable to tobacco smoke[27]. One cannot remain indifferent to the economic costs, and above all to the cost of life.

Monopoly (in Italy) earns from the sale of cigarettes and from gambling, which leverages consumers through subtle mechanisms, or by advertising the idea of a better life thanks to the "scratch and lose" which, with their captivating slogans ("Tourist forever", "a boat of money", etc.), in moments of strong social pressures such as the economic recession and the financial crisis attract people as a magnet who, seeing no other solutions, hope to win at the game to change their life situation. Of course, there is no shortage of addiction campaigns by the Ministry of Health: how many beautiful advertisements! But these initiatives are then

---

[27] F. Romano et al., "Il trattamento del tabagismo: costi e ricadute", «Tabaccologia», 2010, 1, 30-41. http://www.tabaccologia.it/PDF/1_2010/6_012010.pdf

completely erased by actions against the citizens' health, such as the sale of cigarettes and gambling. These mechanisms will bring gold bribes into the pockets of a few but, in my opinion, they are very questionable. How to sell gluten-containing food to those with celiac disease, and then treat it. Everyone knows that the first thing to do is change your diet!

Now, you know how this convoluted mechanism works. The only solution to not fall for it is not to smoke but eliminate the cigarette! Remember that smokers contribute to personal, social and environmental damage.[28] Do not take it as an indictment but as an information. Another point of view to help you better understand and be aware, and not guilty, of your choices and the results they can generate. Those who buy cigarettes are responsible for their choice. You can make conscious choices and know that, in addition to being good for your body, you can contribute to the wellness of society and planet. In conclusion, if you make the decision to use the "electronic cigarette", carry it out with conviction, with the intention of finally freeing yourself. On the other hand, that swing between the "electronic cigarette" and a few "puffs" on the classic cigarette is not good. If you use the "electronic cigarette", you cannot touch another cigarette. Otherwise, go ahead and smoke. Or…

The cigarette substitutes

Cigarette substitutes (such as patches and chewing gum), according to what the same term indicates, "replace" it. Pay attention to it because this is nothing more than an advertising manipulation. To replace, in its common sense, means "to use instead of". If you use an external substance or device in place of the cigarette, you will end up becoming addicted to the substitute as well, sooner or later. The most suitable and correct term would be to support, not substitute. Therefore, the "substitutes" for the cigarette must be used smartly and only if there is a strong need, because they must support the person in the cessation. In addition, the use of "substitutes" must provide for a gradual decrease in dosage, as well as an intelligent management of administration times. Only if used in this way can the substitute offer valid support.

---

[28] G. Mangiaracina, "Impatto multidimensionale del Tabacco su individuo, società e ambiente", Convegno Nazionale "Tabacco e ambiente", enea, 13 giugno 2012. http://www.enea.it/it/comunicare-la-ricerca/events/tabacco-ambiente_13giu12/Mangiaracina.pdf

I specify that it will not be nicotine substitutes that will make you quit smoking, but that the result will depend on you. Do what you feel, apply advice, tips and exercises, train yourself to create a new reality. Substitutes can only be an incentive, a support. They can be a first step in strengthening the decision to finally break free.

Focus

Imagine a mechanic who must perform precision work on a car, or a computer scientist who works out a new program. If they are smokers, it is very likely that before starting to work they light a cigarette "in order to focus". In both situations, smoking becomes a sort of attention accelerator, amplifies the focus, helps the process. Nicotine increases attention; it also stimulates the production of dopamine, which generates a feeling of wellness. So, here is the connection cigarette = more attention. Does it really happen or is it just a belief?

Well friends, it really happens, and it is our ability to generate connections in each situation and make them snap automatically to the repetition of the stimulus, in our case with the cigarette. However, this is to your advantage because it means that you have been able to create a mental and physical connection as well as between the cigarette and the performance, you can do it with something healthy. So, do it now! Anyone who smokes, whenever a situation arises in which concentration is required, feels the stimulus of the cigarette. In fact, the use of cigarettes in performance situations, which therefore require commitment, attention and can also generate stress, acts as an activator, and / or support, and / or reward for the performance itself. It is important to unhinge this connection. From now on, should you feel the desire for a cigarette in a performance situation, try to do this:

1. Replace the cigarette with (preferably) an empowering action towards your wellness. By action we mean exercising, reading, writing, meditating; it can also be just thinking productively. You could also eat fruit, drink a smoothie or just water. You are free to choose from your enhancement options. It is possible to carry out the actions that require your participation only in the pre- and post-performance phase, hardly during. In the latter, on the other hand, I suggest you listen to the music you like best and that most stimulates you towards a better performance. I also suggest the use of fragrances, which are very

powerful synaptic activators. Avoid nicotine substitutes and surrogates if possible.

2. Enjoy the moment: make sure you enter a state of mind of wellness and pleasure, the real one, not the artificial one of when you smoked. Focusing on your desired state will help you feel better and faster.

The challenge is to create a new successful scheme. Much conscious repetition is required for the new mechanism to consolidate; you must consider and perform it many times mechanically to turn it into an automatic action, thus transforming itself into your new ritual. Many people have told me that this training phase has been fun. Make your training fun and it will become a productive habit!

David's story

David always told me to be lazy; he did not like going to the gym and playing sports at all. Once he decided to quit smoking, he began the correct diet for him, even beginning to train. He chose a new ritual that for a lazy person like him was a real challenge: to the stimulation of the cigarette, he had to perform ten push-ups on the arms. Do like him, choose your new ritual. Make it matched to another goal, such as having an athletic, energized, and healthy body. I have found that when a person associates a commitment with the achievement of two goals at the same time, a lot of motivation and energy is generated. It is like having a double engine that pushes: if one of the two engines slows down, there is still the other. Do you understand how powerful this decision is? Predictably, David first performed the chosen exercise with a little effort, but after about ten days he began to enjoy it. The healthy taste of wellness. After the first month, only one message passed through his mind: "You're doing well, your muscles are growing, you love yourself, you feel great." All real and concrete aspects; he was not doing a self-convincing campaign. David saw measurable results both quantitatively and qualitatively. In addition to the mere physical improvement, he felt full of energy even on an inner level and he strengthened himself day after day in his work performances as well (he was a salesman). The association of two goals, one of which is certainly measurable (in this case physical training, but you could also decide to start redecorating the house or learning something new) will help you quit smoking because you will see a gradual growth for yourself. but concrete, and therefore you will not feel tempted to abandon your intent because of prejudices, personal impressions and excuses.

Doing so, David was able to replace - or rather to erase - old habits with new, healthy and fun, much more satisfying and exciting ones than the cigarette. He just wanted to improve day by day, to go further; and he did all this even while he was working. A bit like it had happened with cigarettes over time, he felt the need to increase the dose. With healthy and regular habits such as playing sports, a satisfying sex life, good nutrition, you have the same psychological effect (feeling of wellness) of the cigarette, since all these activities physiologically favour the production of endogenous substances such as dopamine, serotonin and beta endorphins, our internal "drugs" that make us feel good. The most important aspect is that with healthy habits, unlike the use of external drugs such as nicotine, the natural mechanism of production of these substances by our body is re-established, a mechanism that the cigarette affects and inhibits.

Surely you are wondering how David could do the push-ups while he was with a client. If the thought of the cigarette was faint, he put it off. But if the thought of the cigarette was strong, he would ask permission, he would go to the toilet and do push-ups. He must have been crazy, anti-conformist, against the tide - I do not know how to define him - but he managed to stick to his own personal program. He planned and carried it forward consistently, that this upset his daily life. This is a good example of a person who trains daily for a result, with commitment and discipline.

Even today, David practices physical activity every day because it helps him feel good, inside and out. The smoking stimulus has disappeared, because it has been replaced with an empowering ritual. You too can choose to practice an activity that improves you, aimed at achieving a motivating goal. As David did with his new and healthy habit: training every day.

Now it's up to you!

Which wellness-oriented empowering practices could you activate in place of the cigarette? Make a short list of possibilities:

Now you can do it, change the scheme!

Maybe these are things you have already thought and written. Thinking more deeply strengthens you. What is the urge to smoke? How do you recognize him? What happens in you? What sensation do you feel? Is it an image? What gives you the urge? In what situations does this happen? Try to anticipate when the stimulus is about to activate, to predict it before it reaches maximum intensity:

_____

_____

_____

Now enter the possible alternatives and choose the most valid ones with which to replace the cigarette.

_____

_____

_____

Set a goal to achieve. Work out your schedule. Progressively monitor the improvements and enjoy the result:

_____

_____

_____

For the next 45 days, put your program into practice.

Mark the deadline on a calendar and tick the days until completion. If you want, you can extend your calendar by setting new deadlines, you are free to do as you prefer. But the most important thing is that you often remind yourself that you are learning a new good habit.

The structure of wellness

Habit and success

Coaching people who have achieved successful results in their wellness, both avid smokers who have definitively freed themselves from cigarettes, and non-smokers who are attentive to their wellness, I was able to extrapolate the structure of thoughts, emotions and actions, therefore also of the beliefs that have enabled them to achieve their goals.

By making this structure yours from now on, you will get the desired result, you will be free too. I've noticed that people who are better off, who know about wellness think in similar terms, do similar things and get wellness results. So, let's see how to learn to think effectively and make it a habit.

Wellness needs attention and habit; it is not a coincidence. People who live well are used to doing it, regardless of their social status. It is not an effort, they always do. Even the condition in which you find yourself is a habit, whatever it is. This concept is applicable to all life areas, indiscriminately.

Charles Duhigg writes from the book The Power of Habits[29]:

> «First there is a signal, a switch that tells our brain to go into automatic mode and which habit to use. Then there is the routine, which can be physical, emotional or mental. Finally, there is gratification, based on which our brain decides whether a certain routine is worth memorizing. Over time this circle - signal, routine, gratification - becomes more and more automatic; signal and gratification intertwine with each other to induce a strong sense of expectation and craving, that is, need. And finally, whether it happens in a cold MIT laboratory or in the garage of your home, the habit is born».

---

[29] C. Duhigg, *op. cit.*

Habit determines what we are today. What we do repeatedly, every day, becomes what we call "natural". Being natural and spontaneous is, paradoxically, synonymous with habit. Habit is so deeply rooted that it becomes an irreplaceable part of our existence, whether it is positive, or rather, aimed at wellness, or negative, oriented towards self-destruction. The orientation towards well-being is the basis of the habits of people who love each other and are committed to staying fit from all points of view. These people turn new behaviours into new habits, with commitment.

The secret is to do what you want to happen.

What you would like it to be. Do only and exclusively what lead you to achieve a desired and concrete result. Eliminate everything else.

The three main areas

Improvement encompasses three areas:

1. The area of the body, which includes nutrition and physical activity.
2. The area of the mind, which includes thoughts and beliefs.
3. The area of behaviour, which includes techniques and strategies, actions to do and not to do.

For each of these areas ask yourself these three simple questions:

1. What do you already do that is useful and functional?
2. What do you do that is not useful or even harmful?
3. What could you do from now to improve? What it should be and the first action?

Create tables by separating what is useful from what is not. Then organize a calendar with set times and write down what you need to do for each area. Always keep it with you, on a piece of paper or on your mobile phone, although personally I would recommend you write in pen on a notepad because it is more effective. Look at it in the morning and keep the important points in mind.

Imagine how you will conduct your day by mentally following all the steps and anticipating the satisfaction you will derive from them.

Body

According to the ancient wisemen, the body is the temple of the soul. For this reason, it should be taken care of in all its aspects. What do you already do to take care of your body? What do you do instead that is not useful or even harmful? What could you do from now to improve?

- Healthy eating: read books on the subject or go to a nutritionist. The saying is true: "Tell me how you eat, and I'll tell you who you are."

- Physical activity: be followed by a professional, join the gym or start a light physical activity and practice it regularly. There are very good, free training videos that you can find on YouTube with exercises of as little as 15 minutes a day that you can perform at home in a simple and effective way.

- Aesthetic care: try the massages, there are also offers around at low prices. Use skin creams. Treat yourself to the best.

Mind

What are you already doing useful and functional to better manage your time? Can you organize the time dedicated to work efficiently? Do you dedicate time to your passions or simply to relax? What do you do instead that is not useful or even counterproductive? What could you do from now to improve?

- TAKE TIME FOR YOURSELF: find a moment of your own, in which you think only of yourself: a walk by the sea, good music, a movie you like, a good book. Your mind needs it more than you can imagine. Even simply of silence.

- CONCENTRATE YOUR WORK IN SOME PART OF THE DAY: for example from 8.00 to 12.00, stop. Then, dedicate yourself to something else, to a hobby, to sport but not to work. Concentrated work is done better, and the pressure is so high that you keep the maximum effort.

By giving yourself a time limit you get two results: the first, you will do better; the second, you will avoid the stress of excessively prolonged activity. "But work relaxes me," you might tell me. Nonsense! Too much work is an excuse for not thinking about your life. That is a form of addiction too. Those who are comfortable with themselves know how to alternate between work and relaxation. "But I can't do it, I'm an employee and I'm not free to do what I want," another might argue. These are excuses too. Organizing and concentrating work does not mean acting at will but giving oneself very precise and rigid rules. What can you do? Simple. Based on the time you have available, concentrate your work in a few hours, commit to making the most of it and dedicate the remaining time to yourself. Working is important, but even more important is dedicating time to your wellness. People who focus their work live much better, achieve their goals and feel satisfied.

- ORGANIZATION. Who is good, manages everything well? A place for everything in its place. Take a weekly schedule and organize the week ahead with it, entering the activities of the three areas. The night before, mentally retraces the next day, to be clear on what and how to manage the next day.

Emotions and Behaviours

What do you already do to listen to your emotions? Do you take care of your relationships? What do you do instead that is not useful or even harmful? What could you do from now to improve?

- Listen to your feelings and emotions. Identify the part of the body they are associated with. Name what you hear. Those who live in the name of wellness have this ability. For some it is innate, but it still needs to be trained.

- After identifying a specific emotion, write down a behaviour to be adopted in response to that emotion. It would be better if it were different from how you usually "react" to that emotion, you must act. Study it at the table.

- Maintain relationships. Your relationships are very important. You may not be able to completely avoid some people, but you can certainly spend more time with the people who make you feel good. Spend your time with people you can improve with. Hang out with people who care about their health, who are fine and want to get better. Stay with happy people. If you think they do not exist, I am sorry to tell you that you hang out with the wrong people. We tend to hang out with people like us. So, we hardly hang out with people who can improve us. There are friendships that drive you to improve surround. It is not easy to find them, and it is not easy to hang out with them. At first you will experience a feeling of discomfort because you will feel behind them. However, this is the only way to improve. The environment is very important.

- Learn to recognize emotions in others. Observe the people you meet, try to empathize with them, recognize their emotions and give them a name. Successful people have this great quality: they recognize others' moods and know how to respect them to create a better environment. Later, we will delve into the emotions related to smoking and you will learn to modify them, anticipate them and create new habits.

When do we get free?

This question is difficult! Please, answer! When do you get rid of the cigarette? When will you know you are cigarette free? You do not. And you will never know if you wait for something to happen, an external confirmation. It is not like one day you get a halo because you have quit smoking. If you try to understand and see the change with your eyes, it will not happen, or rather it will happen, but you will tend not to see it. Or, if you see it, you will most likely not interpret it in favour of the decision you have made, which is to quit smoking. I can guarantee you that if you listen to your feelings, you will feel that you have changed, you will notice even the smallest change. Change is felt.

However, if you are looking for a clear sign that you are not a smoker, then look in the mirror. Do it now and you will immediately notice the difference; the appearance of the skin in fact improves after only three days without cigarettes. Is this enough to understand that you are no longer a smoker? Not enough, is it?

I knew it! The problem is that you experience this change as if you are waiting around the corner for something that can confirm the "rule": "I will never stop". Until then, you will tell yourself and others that you are still not so sure if you have succeeded. The change comes from within. Maybe you already have a new feeling or maybe you already experience relationships differently. Do you feel something different inside of you? When did you smoke your last cigarette? Then, you are already a non-smoker. Just repeat, repeat and repeat again the exercises in this book and automatically your new program will be wellness.

The language you use is fundamental. Often the smoker repeats himself in his mind: "If I don't smoke for six months it means that I won't smoke anymore", "If I don't smoke for a year it means that I have definitively quit", etc. All excuses, all wrong messages, all resistances to change, bad habits. Keep doing the exercises and reading, don't obsess about having to stop, concentrate your commitment on following all the exercises in the book in a focused way. Immediately after the last cigarette, you are non-smokers. It can happen even now. This is the rule, the most powerful belief:

After the last cigarette, you are already a non-smoker!

Test yourself

If you still feel confused, help yourself with this exercise. We met it at the end of the previous chapter, but I invite you to repeat it even now, it is very powerful.

Exercise

1. Imagine smoking your last cigarette. Use all your imagination. Concentrate, light it, this is the last time. Visualize the scene in your mind as if it were a movie that flows before your eyes, imagine all the details in a vivid and intense way: the embers igniting, the sensation of smoke descending into your lungs and then thrown out, no to consuming your last cigarette.

2. Imagine now taking the pack with the remaining cigarettes (remember that the last cigarette is a choice, not a constraint because the last one left in the pack or at home) and break it into a thousand pieces, crush it, with all the anger that

you would reserve for who or what has hurt you, has ruined part of your life, for those who told you they loved you but hurt you. Pour on the pack of cigarettes that anger that we often turn against ourselves. Now the package is destroyed, forever and permanently.

Throw away what's left in the garbage can.

3. Now, you can breathe deeply and when you visualize yourself in the act of throwing the package forever, repeat aloud "That's enough!" or any other phrase that refers to the decision of freedom. While doing this, press PIDX.

4. Project your imagination into a moment or a situation of your future as a non-smoker, a scene full of well-being and happiness. You are in great shape, surrounded by the people you love. What do you see? What smells and sounds do you perceive? Are you perhaps at the sea? At a party? Or have you just returned home from work, tired but satisfied? Imagine your favourite situation as it were a movie, enjoy it fully as you breathe deeply and hold PIDX.

Repeat for 5 times.

If you return to the present with a feeling of relief and the desire to give your best, to reach the new goals that we are formulating together, I congratulate you! You are on the right path, let's continue!

Talk to your stimulus

Any question or doubt that comes to your mind, I propose another very powerful exercise.

Exercise

If you feel like smoking a cigarette, the first thing to do is... don't smoke it! Of course, this is obvious, you will tell me. But now I'm going to teach you to familiarize yourself with a technique that will make a difference. I'll let you talk to the symptom!

1. Accept the stimulus. Remember that the symptom always has something to tell you. What comes from us always has a positive function. Nothing that comes to us is born with the intention of harming us.

2. Talk to "him". Now, imagine having in front of you, sitting on a chair, Mr. Stimulus, and have a chat with him. Follow the questions and address them to your stimulus as if he were sitting in front of you, in flesh and blood. Then give him time to respond. With a little patience and training you will get the first results. I know, it's not a walk in the park, but this exercise, with a little commitment, has helped many of the people I followed in coaching because it provides a key to reframe the problems and give them a new meaning.[30]

Let's see the exercise step by step:

1. Ask your stimulus: "Do you want to talk to me?" Yes/No? If he answers No, give him some time. He must trust you after you have neglected him for too long. Let him understand that it is important to you.

2. Say, "I accept you; you are part of me. Thanks for existing, I know you want my good".

3. Ask, "What is your positive function?" Make it specific. What it protects you from, why it does it, etc. Give him time, if he doesn't answer, repeat the question.

4. Ask, "What can I do to have your intention respected and propel me towards wellness?"

If you cannot answer immediately, do not be discouraged! It is difficult to question who we are, what we want and why, yet it is necessary to bring out the best in ourselves. Trust yourself and your feelings, stay anchored to the answers. Engage in answering, give yourself permission to do so. The answers may not arrive immediately but use the strategy of repeating the questions as soon as you can. You will hear the answer emerge and tell you the truth.

A new way of life

Diet

Remedy and solution rhymes with a new wellness-oriented lifestyle. The suggestions that I propose to you serve to facilitate the journey, but they are not

---

[30] R. Bandler, J. Grindler, La ristrutturazione. La programmazione neurolinguistica e la trasformazione del significato, Astrolabio-Ubaldini, 1983 Roma.

medical prescriptions. If you see fit, consult your doctor, dietician or nutritionist before putting them into practice. Nutrition indicated to facilitate smoking cessation and detoxification: foods rich in fibre, whole grains (barley, spelled, etc.), vegetables, fruit, water are always useful and especially in the first month.

These foods will help you in digestion and to go to the body avoiding feelings of discomfort. You will feel that you have more energy, and they will also help you maintain your weight. Discipline is the key word to get the result you want, coupled with motivation. You can do it, you will not starve, on the contrary. We are used to a disastrous diet. We eat everything and badly. Instead, aim for quality rather than quantity. Without going into the merits of the individual diets, below you will find some valid suggestions that have allowed all my clients to maintain their ideal weight and to lose weight.

- The first three days: water, juices, fruit and vegetables, whole grains. Only these.

- From the fourth day you can add the fish. Avoid meat, fried food, alcoholic beverages, and exciting drinks like tea and coffee for at least 10 days. Also avoid decaf; at the beginning, the cigarette is always anchored to taste and therefore also to smells.

- Eat five times a day (in general take advantage of fibre: vegetables, whole grains).

- The first month it is better to use milk and egg proteins rather than meat. In general, prefer white meats and fish and reduce the consumption of sausages and red meats to maintain optimal physical shape. I must add, however, that for some, the intake of milk can cause various problems of intolerance, so always relate the suggestions you find here to your personal situation.

Personally, I no longer take animal milk, I prefer vegetable, oat, spelled and soy milk.

- Drink 2 to 4 litres of water a day for the first month. And if you continue to do so in the following months, so much the better. But be careful not to overload your kidneys! Drink in sips, not 3 litres at once!

- Also consider the possibility of approaching vegetarian cuisine: you may discover many pleasant, tasty and healthy foods, but always get advice from an expert on the subject.

- Start meals with a salad: it will be very pleasant. Prepare appetizing and tasty salads.

- Chew more and eat more slowly; enjoy the food.

Obviously, you can eat everything. Only in the first month will you have to commit yourself and sacrifice some of your eating habits.

Always continue to prefer nutritious and healthy foods.

Physical activity

Physical activity, along with a healthy diet, plays a crucial role with repercussions on the quality of emotional and working life, on everything. Feeling good in your body means feeling good in your mind. Sport has multiple benefits: psycho-physical balance; greater energy and discharge of accumulated tensions; new relationships; widespread feeling of strength and wellness. Physical activity in fact stimulates the production of endorphins which, as mentioned before, are the internal "drug" we have and that we can produce whenever we want. In fact, there is also abstinence from training, which is a healthy form of addiction. In short, we are better off doing physical activity. However, regarding sport and physical activity, resistance can be triggered. Even though the phrase "I want to get better" is on everyone's lips, few are willing to commit. Someone will come up with the usual excuses:

"I don't have time", "How can I do with everything I have to do?", "I'm tired in the evening", "I'm lazy", "I live well anyway", etc. These people do not want to get better, deep down they do not really want it. Yes, I like to provoke, but it is also reality. Prove me the opposite, let me see that it is not so! I will be glad I am wrong. Free from the cigarette, the smoker has 1-2 hours more during the day than previously spent smoking. It also applies to you! Think about which sport you might be interested in dance, martial arts, soccer, volleyball, swimming, running. Any activity you enjoy, connects you with other people, helps you to improve as an individual. By doing sport you train your discipline! You will get amazing results. By engaging in physical activity and a healthy diet, you will discover that you have much more time available than you think. You will begin to create a balance in your daily life, finding spaces to dedicate to yourself, to your family, to work. And you will be fine, finally free from the cigarette you will never think about anymore. Because when you feel good, the rest does not matter.

The butterfly is so busy flying that it no longer thinks about being a caterpillar.

Get involved in some activity or hobby

Passion is why we exist. The desire to get up and think about something from the first moment of the day. Wishing the moment in which to be able to dedicate oneself to one's passion is one of the most pleasant expectations. How many passions have you hidden under the carpet like dust? Yet your passions still exist, albeit under the blanket of daily commitments and worries. Take your time and dream more. Imagine having time, money and whatever else is useful to be able to practice your passion. What passions would you like to resume or experience?

List all the passions - the ones that excite you as soon as you think about it - that you would like to take back. Remember that passions are a different thing from sport, which implies a particular discipline and commitment. They may coincide, but what I want is that when you think about your passion, you feel carefree; even if you don't practice it for a few months, you don't feel guilty and you miss nothing. In sport, however, it is well known that as soon as you stop practicing, you lose the physical condition achieved. If you love painting pictures, it doesn't matter if you stop for a while. What you have achieved you see hanging, it remains. Clear? Make a list, dream a little, even things you've never done and would like to try, then choose at least one and start it despite everything. Do it for you! Give yourself this gift. You deserve it! You are deserving of the best.

Make a list of your passions:

_____

_____

Change habits to feel good

Face the difficulties

If at times it seems difficult to understand which path to take, which choice to make, it is because we focus on the situation and on others and divert attention from ourselves. Instead, focus only on yourself and your wellness. Only in this way will you be able to modify the outside world in such a way as to attract the most suitable situations and people. However, this will only happen if you have worked on an inner level.

If you change, everything around you changes. People prefer to suffer situations, they try to "soften them" by comparing them to worse: "It gets worse!". Cabbage, there is even better: not the comparison with others, but your best. What's your best, what do you want from life? What is the dream of your life? Dreaming and acting is what you need to feel good. As children we knew how to dream and growing up, they deprived us of the ability to do so. They told us that you must stay "with your feet on the ground". Yes, it's true, you need to set yourself realistic, concrete goals and not useless longings, but it is one thing to keep your feet on the ground, it is another to stay planted, watching life go by. There is nothing to sweeten. I often notice that people read books, participate in personal growth courses, devote themselves to spirituality not to improve themselves but to seek confirmation of their beliefs and to be able to say that others are wrong. They seek some relief. They do all this as if they are taking a pain reliever. Face the difficulties. People tend to avoid dealing with delicate situations, fearing that they will suffer further. Yet in doing so they remain tied to the wrong things or people, which make them feel bad. You cannot do it; you cannot think of changing things by staying within the system that continues to feed your malaise. Here is the reason for the cigarette: it is the only thing - or one of the few - that gives you the idea of being able to exercise control or to be able to modify or manage situations to some extent. You convince yourself that it is you who smoke and that in this no one can command or decide for you. A bit like getting a tattoo, the meaning of which is not only what is attributed to it, but it is also an explicit message that says: "It's my body and here I decide!". Strive to change the "avoidance pattern". When situations arise that you are tempted to back down, avoid avoiding. When you avoid, the difficulties are amplified more and more.

Mental reconditioning

Imagine going back in time again; you have already been there at the beginning of our journey together, but now you can change the state of things and make a difference. Go back to the moment you picked up the Cigarette (the first one). Here, you are there that you hold it in your hand, you turn it on but just before you can bring it to your mouth and start smoking it, the video of your future starts, with you smokers as the protagonists. Watch the film until the end. Look at it several times and write below what you don't like, how you see yourself and if you used to smoke, and what. Write as much as you can, as much detail as possible.

How is the movie of your life as a smoker? How do you see yourself? What was the use of smoking for you?

_____

_____

_____

Now, from the past, take the door of time that will allow you to go straight to your last day of life on this earth. Turn around and see from this perspective how you spent your life as a smoker until old age. Watch the scenes that flow several times, from the moment you started until the last day. What would you not do again? What would you change? What was the use of smoking, what prevented you? How would you behave if you could go back to today when you are reading this book? Visualize everything you would change in your life including smoking, relationships, friendships, whatever you want. If you could go back in time, what would you change about your life as a smoker?

_____

_____

_____

Now, follow these directions and repeat them every day. He writes on a piece of paper and always carry them with you. Stop during the day and reread them. Every day, from now on.

Everyday:

1. What are my goals today?

2. What goals have I achieved?

3. What is beautiful in my life? List at least 5 things.

4. What can I improve in my life? At least 3 things.

5. Statement: "Today I am freer than yesterday, and stronger. Today I will improve so that tomorrow will be stronger than today. I am free and full of well-being now. The result I want is coming, it is getting closer every day".

6. Imagine yourself in your ideal condition, at your top.

In everyday life, with friends, in relationships, at work, in everything. Think strongly about your ideal condition, as if you have already reached it. Review this movie at least 2 times every day, in the morning and in the evening. Make it a habit.

Awareness – Constant Effort – Verification

A small commitment

Be careful! I'm not asking you to make big changes, but a small but constant commitment. But first you must become aware of your habits, edifying. By habits I mean both what you do and what you do not usually do. What do you do when you get up in the morning? How do you move? In what order do you do things? All of these are habits. For example, I do 20 minutes of training immediately after waking up. This is a healthy and empowering habit. I am not obsessed with it or and I do not force myself to do it; it is, in fact, a habit.

In the summer, I change some habits, change my routine and do different things: I reduce my training, go to the beach, take a period of relaxation. I keep running and exercising, but less often and not in the morning; I prefer the evening, when it's cooler. If you don't do sports, if you are lazy, you are used to not training. In this case, you may decide to start doing some physical activity: a course in the gym that you like, long walks, a bit of running, or just some exercises at home.

Make a list of your habits:

_____

_____

_____

Pick one of these habits, the one you think might be easiest to change, and work on it. Change it! Replace it with an empowering habit, which aims at your wellness. It is not about doing great things; it could just be reading a book. Starting from simple things greatly increases success and reinforces the conviction of being able to realize the goals you set yourself. It helps you to be more effective and determined. Train the determination muscle. But know that you must complete what you have undertaken. Also for this reason, start with small changes. You will always go on growing. This is a habit too. There is also the tendency to postpone things among the habits, until they become so big that they can no longer manage them and are forced to cope with an increase in difficulties, when they could have been anticipated. How many times has this happened to you? Yet always remember habits determine actions. Actions crystallize into habits. Habits determine identity. Do you know the moment when you dedicate yourself to cleaning up your room? Experience a pleasant sensation both while doing it and when you have the result in front of your eyes. A feeling of external cleanliness and internal order. In fact, you are often driven almost compulsively to tidy up the other rooms or the car and sometimes you even want to put your life in order. When you activate yourself towards wellness, you will gradually be overwhelmed by it, and you will feel pushed to put order in all areas of your life. If there is something you put off, like cleaning your room or fixing up the garage, force yourself to do it now. After you will be taken by the desire to put something else in order. You will come to want to put your health in order and free yourself from the cigarette will no longer be a goal, but a natural consequence, to amplify the wellness that has been generated. A cascade effect.

What could your new empowering habits be?

_____

_____

_____

Proceed with one habit at a time. Consider it a workout. When you have changed the old habit and installed the new one, you can change another one. It will help you to create a daily agenda in which to insert the new habit to be installed alongside your usual commitments.

Muscle Response Test

Now your left hand represents the whole negative of the cigarette. Join the index and thumb of the left hand (PISX) and think about all the rottenness that you have connected to the cigarette in this path. Visualize the scenes, listen and relive the connected sensations, recall their smell, taste, and put everything on the left side of your mental screen. After this, let's move on to the positive part. Reactivate all the empowering, positive images that you connected by joining the index and thumb of the right hand (PIDX).

View images and recover empowering sensations; breathe deeply as you retrace the scenes of your future. You perceive new and pleasant tastes and smells (if it is not easy to connect pleasant smells and tastes, imagine biting a good Sicilian lemon). Do you feel that your breathing is free and different than before? Increase and amplify the energy coming from the right hand. Imagine everything on the right side of the screen in front of you. Now comes the proof of trials, an effective test that never fails when done correctly. It is called the "Muscle Response Test". Before putting it into practice, read through to learn how it works. The aim is to learn to communicate directly with your unconscious, with the unconscious part that manages each of us[31]. The answer he will give you will be clear. Your mind will not give it, your body will guide you. It is a muscular

_____

[31] R. Dujany, Teoria e impiego pratico della Kinesiologia Applicata, 2000 Milano, p. 32.

response. It works. It never fails. It will communicate your unconscious "decision" to you.

> Exercise
>
> Press hard forefinger and thumb of the left hand (negative, limiting sensations, scene on the left side of the screen).
>
> Good. Now, a circle has been created; join the thumb and forefinger of the right hand (positive, empowering sensations and scene on the right side of the screen) by passing them inside the circle of the left hand as if to form a "∞". For the moment, don't do the exercise, just read it; I'm going through it step by step to make it clearer.
>
> The circles formed by the right and left hand are linked together. Also tighten the circle of the right hand tightly, very tightly. Both with strength. Try to detach the rims and you will feel some resistance. Are you there? Very good. Your left is identified with "no", your right with "yes"!
>
> Out loud, ask this question to your unconscious: "Have I decided to be free forever and finally free myself from the cigarette, to live a happy life?". Forcefully pull your hands in the opposite direction as if to break the union. Squeeze both the right- and left-hand hoops tightly. Pull as hard as you can. Break the chain. If the ring formed by the thumb and index finger of the left hand remains closed, the answer is "no". In this case, you will have to continue reading and doing the exercises in order to focus even more. Don't be disappointed: it can happen, it is no coincidence that I have reiterated several times that it takes training. If, on the other hand, the ring formed by the thumb and index finger of the right hand remains intact, then the answer is a full "yes". The fingers that opened could not withstand the opposite force. Your unconscious has clearly communicated the decision to you. Be happy with it!
>
> Please try again for confirmation. Keep exercising. Reread everything when you want or think it is useful. Remember that it must become a habit.
>
> Test and calibrate the exercise
>
> Before running the test, it must be calibrated. It is important to be fully aware of how it works and its validity. Before you begin, take a good deep breath. Cross your fingers together, two linked rings, as mentioned before. The left hand means no (addiction), the right hand yes (freedom).

Now say, "My name is... (insert your real name)". Notice that the right resists as the fingers of the left open, right?

Try your job now. "I do... (tell the truth)". And the same thing happens. The right wins.

Try again asking other questions, to get an answer from the unconscious.

Now repeat: "My name is... (add a false name)". The left won, right? You have now calibrated the test.

Nobody can influence you. It's the right time: you can do it by asking yourself the question about our path.

Read, reread, and apply this chapter for the next few days. If it comes out "yes" it is the right time to finally be free.

If it turns out *yes*, then rejoice!

I am finally free!

Inhale deeply and repeat 10 times:

I am finally a free person!

8 RECONDITIONING

«Never mistake motion for action»

Ernest Hemingway

If you could go back in time, to the day you tried to smoke, to the day you lit your first cigarette, how would you behave? Imagine the situation, go back to that moment, now you are there. Imagine the moment you are about to light your first cigarette, aware of the fact that you will become the smokers you are today. Now, tell me: would you smoke it, yes or no? There are no shades, yes or no! Very good! If not, we can continue; and rest assured, the change will bring you an increase in wellness.

> Exercise
>
> Now, imagine your life from today to the future. You can visualize the time line in one of two ways: o the time line crosses you (from back to front, fig. A), so that your past is behind you, you are in the present and in front of you is extends the future; or the time line runs in front of you, with the past on your left, the present in the centre and the future on the right (from left to right fig. b). Where do you see your past and your future?

FUTURE

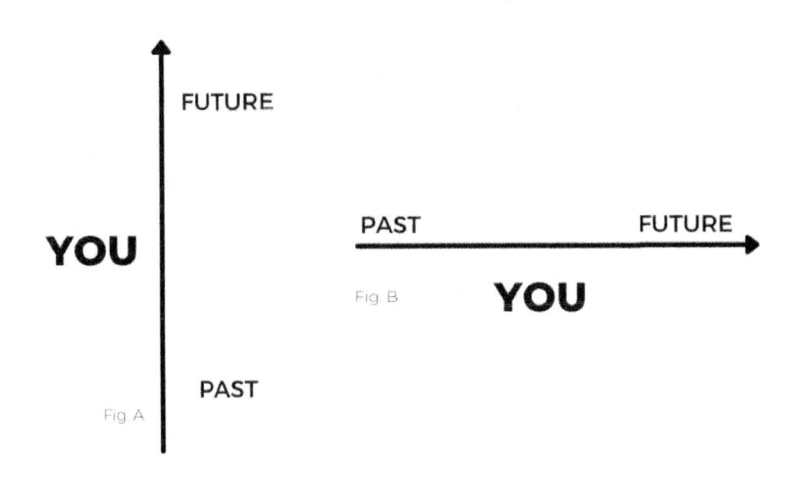

YOU

PAST

Fig. A

PAST ——————— FUTURE

Fig. B **YOU**

Visualize this line in your mind from now until the day you are finally and free from the cigarette. Choose the colour you like best and start colouring, like a coloured beam of light, the time line from now until the appointed day. It can be a date, or even just a point on the line. Colour to the point where you have regained your original energies; you will feel more and more smoke-free: now you are non-smokers and breathe deeply.

As you go along, progressively colour your timeline; inevitably, even if you try to oppose it, the sensation that pushed you towards the cigarette will reduce, while the desire for health on the one hand and the disgust for cigarettes on the other will increase, to the point of indifference. As in a scale, the more the plate of health and wellness goes down because the desire to feel good weighs more, the more the plate of the cigarette rises until it disappears and dissolves completely.

Repeat for 5 times.

Things to do

Once you have become aware and have decided to permanently free yourself from the cigarette, do exactly the following:

- Throw out all supplies of cigarettes. Do not wait to finish the last package, it would be stupid. Do not think it is a waste. When you feel your "inner spring" springing, when you feel a new identity being born in you, throw away all the cigarettes, the tobacco stocks, the papers, the filters, the ashtrays, the lighters, everything that has to do with the cigarette.

Do it as soon as this new awareness arises.

- Clean and perfume your home, car, office. Thoroughly clean the places where you previously smoked and tidy up where clutter used to be desks, bedrooms, wardrobes, etc. These are the first things I suggest you do. Why? By cleaning and perfuming your environment, freeing it from cigarette traces, you eliminate the possibility of stimulation, discourage recovery. These are simple but practical and effective suggestions.

- Change some of your habits. If you filmed yourself with a video camera every morning, you would find that you always do the same things. Even if you do not remember anything about the first half hour of the day, when you go on autopilot. This happens because the neuronal circuits that manage everyday life are now tested, they work with a "Click and go!". As soon as they receive the first input, they are activated automatically; everything else comes by itself.

For example, you get up, wash your face, put on the coffee, go back to the bathroom, then go back to the kitchen, have coffee, have breakfast with milk and biscuits, go back to the bathroom, to the bedroom, get dressed and go out. Obviously, in this series of habits there is perhaps still the cigarette for some of you. It seems that from the first moments of the morning, from the success of this routine or from the onset of some hitch, it is established whether the day will go well or badly. It is no coincidence that it is said: "I got up with a crooked foot!". From now on, pay attention to doing slightly different things from the beginning of your day. You don't have to upset your life and your habits, just a few tricks. Put your waking habits on paper. You will discover that the cigarette is promptly foretold by certain behaviours and thoughts.

For 3 days, take note of your daily actions. *I know it can be tricky as soon as you wake up, however it is important.*

There are patterns that you follow in an organized way that you are not always aware of. As soon as you have a map of the repeated behaviours, you can start modifying them. Put them in succession, because they are tied. Sometimes changing just one or two steps means changing the whole sequence.

Stratagems

- If you are sleeping on a double bed, switch sides. If you sleep on the right, start lying on the left side. If you are not alone and you share a bed with a partner, ask for help and swap places; on the other hand, if you sleep in a single bed, switch your head with your feet.

- Change your place at the table. After lunch, run to brush your teeth.

- Remember that only those who have no passions experience moments of boredom. Search, find, take back your passion. Do what gives you strength and joy. Everything. You will see that there will be no dull moment.

- In times of stress, anger, sadness, apply 1: 4: 2 breathing (explained later).

- If you get the abominable desire to light a cigarette, in addition to practicing the mental exercises you have become experts in, immediately drink a glass of water in at least 6 sips.

Hold the water in your mouth for a moment before swallowing.

- If you are unable to stop despite everything: *a.* Determine in which places and situations you can smoke and those in which you cannot. Make a detailed list. For example, you could choose not to smoke in places such as your home, car, office; or in situations where there are children, or even on certain days of the week such as holidays, odd days. You do. If you have the desire and you are at home, you must not prevent it, you can smoke: the important thing is that you leave the building where you live and smoke down in the courtyard. The balconies and windows are also part of the house. *b.* If you are driving or are in any case aboard a car, you can only smoke as soon as you get off. You can stop and smoke one. And so on in all situations in which you have chosen not to smoke. Follow these guidelines and you will be able to manage the addiction until you quit. *c.* If your own or feel the urge to smoke, do it only in uncomfortable conditions. After smoking, clean the ashtray immediately. Empty it after each cigarette. Day after day you will begin to see the results of your efforts.

From now on, continue to apply these precautions. And remember that you can only smoke when you cannot resist and always respecting the rules, your schedule. This is the last resort, not a permit to do so. Use your intelligence and be honest with yourself.

Techniques

- Stimulate circulation: when you take a shower, alternate cold and hot water to stimulate circulation and thus purify the body more quickly.

- Breathing: do exercises for proper oxygenation of the body. Take a comfortable position, sitting or lying down, and inhale filling the belly and chest in 3"; hold the air for 12" and exhale in 6". You can change the times while always keeping the same 1: 4: 2 ratios.

- 2 times a day, in the morning and in the evening before going to bed, take 10 minutes just for you. Imagine that the air you breathe is of the colour you like the most and it removes the rot deposited starting from the head and descending to the feet by entering your body. Slowly, as you inhale, your body purifies and regenerates itself while exhaling you throw out the toxic residues. Your body becomes cleaner and purer, as good as new with each repetition; your breath is free, you feel strong and present. You feel good. You are in a state of wellness. In order to strengthen it, press the thumb against the index finger of the right hand (PIDX).

- "Timeless": the technique explained in the paragraph you find a little further on, "timeless". After this exercise you feel free, as if the past and bad memories have never existed or have never had an unpleasant meaning. It takes training to become good at using this technique.

    However, as soon as you understand how it works, you will be able to practice it even faster; the faster it is, the more effective it becomes.

- Tidy up and keep clean: regardless of everything, get used to keeping your home, office and car in order. If you think there is no connection with wellness, you are wrong. The place where you live reflects what you have inside. If there is disorder outside, it is also like this inside. Tidy up and keep your environment clean and the same will happen within you. Keep relationships in order and clean up constantly in this area as well. Build around you the ideal and welcoming environment in which everyone would like to live, you are first.

Time distortion exercise

Here is another exercise that will contribute to your wellness. Being in control of the perception of time is one of the greatest powers we have as human beings.

There are not many who know it and know how to consciously put it into practice. The goal is to develop the habit of using your mind in a different way than usual. It is not magic. You already do it every day, you have done it hundreds of thousands of times, but unconsciously. Have you ever been in a car, immersed in your thoughts, finding yourself at home without remembering the road you travelled, the things you saw outside, and you have the feeling that only 10 minutes have passed since departure while there is took an hour? Or to rest for 15 minutes and wake up feeling like you have slept for two hours? Here, these are two examples of time distortion, the same that smokers often reproduce with the use of cigarettes.

By smoking, the smoker manages to leave, entering an altered state, in a parallel world, as if he were dreaming; in that lapse of time the experience built with the mind lives, and not the real one. Time is decided by the subjective internal experience, and not by the external one. Time distortion can also be experienced in reverse, in the sense that you can extend the time of a positive experience and make sure you have the impression that it lasts longer. Usually holidays, moments of relaxation or fun seem to last a short time. They pass quickly, don't they? Now, you can restrict the time when you do not like it and expand it when you like it. It is all a matter of perception; you do not need a cigarette. Leveraging the cigarette is certainly the stupidest and most uneconomical way to do it because you can do it very well by yourself by exercising your mind. I make the exercise easy for you because you must pay attention to how you *naturally* distort your time. Now you just must observe to take control.

Exercise

1. Take your pen and notebook and carry them with you for at least a week, or for as long as you see fit.

2. Choose the moments that are useful for practicing this exercise. It is not limiting; however, you should distinguish between the pleasant moments in which time usually seems to pass quickly and the less pleasant moments in which it never seems to pass.

3. Look at the time, measure the time relative to the chosen situation.

4. Without looking at the clock or relying on time references such as news, television broadcasts or any other temporal link, at the end of each chosen situation (pleasant or not), write in your notebook: the event, the time according to you past, what you thought and how you thought it.

> **Example**
>
> You are having dinner with a pleasant person. Time goes by, you think an hour has passed instead 3 very pleasant hours have passed. This is a distortion.
>
> *Event*: dinner with...
>
> *Perceived Time*: 1 hour (actual 3 hours).
>
> *Thoughts*: In my mind, I imagined a series of very pleasant possible future moments together.

This is a simplification of the exercise in order to have a reference. The important issue is to pay attention to the fact that the various moments can be traced back to two types: pleasant and unpleasant. Very simple. The former pass faster, the others do not. Obviously, it is a perception, yet our perception is our reality. What can you do with the notes? Use them to learn how to replicate this new knowledge in your everyday reality, to restrict time to less pleasant moments and dilate it to more pleasant ones. You will no longer need the cigarette, but only to focus your thoughts and feelings in an intelligent, more aware and productive way. You do not have to learn anything new, because you do it every day. You just must focus your energies on the moment that interests you most. I myself resort to time distortion when I feel the need to rest and have only a few minutes. I will explain what I do. I imagine - I am convinced - that I only have 5 minutes to wake up, when I have half an hour. Initially, I feel anxious thinking that I do not even have time to close my eyes, but immediately after I can relax and fall asleep as if I have no time limit. However, I always wake up within the 30 minutes available with the feeling of having rested much more time. So, I realize to be already satisfied even before I have finished the established sleep cycle.

Find your way to distort time. I warn you, as in everything it takes training. Instead of using the cigarette, train to put yourself in the best mental predisposition so that time passes faster. You could also take your time to do something you really enjoy rather than just thinking about it. You can read a book. Start doing new activities, pick up on things you enjoyed doing. Do whatever you think is useful. Now, you know that time depends on you, not on the clock.

Get used to making decisions

I talked about the habit of *making decisions*. Many are used to suffer, not to decide. The exercise that I propose now will help you to train your determination, even to free yourself from smoking. Be careful! Starting now, you will have to decide every day. A not too demanding decision. What you have been putting off for some time could be an interesting start. This is a short list that I usually give to my patients to stimulate reflection:

- Decide to go and take out the trash.
- Decide to take care of your diet.
- Decide to spend less time on those who only tell you complaints.
- Decide to stop biting your nails.
- Decide to do what you feel and not what you have to do.
- Decide that when you are tired it is best to let go and rest.
- Decide to take a vacation.
- Decide to do the thing you often postpone.
- Decide to finally fix the closet!
- Decide...

Decide you have been putting off for a while and get started. Many smokers try. But they do not really decide. The attempt has failure. Deciding, on the other hand, means eliminating the less useful alternatives and heading towards your goal. Nobody can and must stand in your way. Decide with your head. Does anyone always tell you what is right for you? You decide to choose. But, how to do it? In order to decide, you must listen to your body as well as your thoughts. I am not suggesting that you do whatever you feel like doing and want. It is not smart to disrespect other people, it is smart to respect yourself. This is only possible if you decide with your own head. When you feel forced to do something, this series of questions can be helpful: "Is this what I want?", "What do I really want?", "What do I need now?", "If I did this how would I feel?", "What else would make me feel good?", "If I were free to choose, would I do it?", "Is it useful for my goal?". Through these simple questions you will be able to understand what is good for you, what you desire. Take the time to decide for yourself. If you do not decide, you are doing something that others have chosen for you. Decision is like a muscle: the more you train it, the stronger it gets. Start easily and increase the load as you understand the mechanism and your decision muscle gets stronger. Imagine the muscle that grows day after day because you train constantly. Just to be clear, you do not have to decide to finish the whole book to get rid of the cigarette, you can do it first. Or decide to read the next paragraph. The next sentence. Small decisions that together open a new path.

The "timeless"

Every day, each of us is occupied with thousands of thoughts (according to some statistics more than 60,000 a day!), 32 which distract us from the present moment, taking us back to the past to mull over what we have not achieved and/or achieved and on that that we have been denied or that we could have done; or by projecting ourselves into the future, to "hope" that one day something will change.

> Exercise
>
> Sit down in a quiet place. Relax totally, do not think in any way about the passing of time. Try to clear your mind of any thoughts. If it helps, fix your gaze on one point. Otherwise, you can close your eyes. As soon as a thought arises and distracts you from the present, bring your attention back to the here and now and breathe deeply. After 10 minutes, open your eyes. How do you feel now?
>
> When you are completely relaxed, you can move on to the next phase of the exercise.
>
> Repeat: "I am a non-smoker!"
>
> How does it feel?

---

32 C. Boni, "Avete mai provato a contare quanti pensieri in un giorno siamo in grado di fare? Qualcuno pare abbia provato a farlo...", 05/03/2010. https://salutebenessere.wordpress.com/2010/03/05/avete-mai-provato-a-contare-quanti-pensieri-in-un-giorno-siamo-in-grado-di-fare-qualcuno-pare-abbia-provato-a-farlo/

Visualize your funeral as a smoker, as if it had happened in the past (not your funeral, I am referring to the funeral of the smoker in you. Imagine it as if you were sitting on the outside.):

Visualize your rebirth to date and repeat: "I am a non-smoker, free from smoke. I've never smoked!" How do you feel?

As you repeat this repeatedly, savouring the sensation, press the thumb and forefinger of your right hand (PIDX). Anchor the feeling. From now on, the only feeling you will have been that from birth to today you have always been free from cigarettes. Always free. Whoever frees himself from something feels inside as if he had never been a prisoner.

Who are you? Who do you want to become? Do this exercise until automatically, magically and strangely, the natural response arrives from the unconscious: "I am a non-smoker, I have never smoked!". You feel it inside, so it is true. If you believe it, you will feel like you have never smoked. This becomes your reality. Because reality is what you live inside, not what happens outside.

The worst that could have happened to you

Our journey together comes to an end. We are towards the end of the book, but at the beginning of a new life, maybe already free from the cigarette. If you really decide to permanently eliminate the cigarette, to be better than before, I want to clarify that the next 30 days will be a catastrophe for you, for your family, for your friends, for your work, for everything. You will feel angry, sad, disappointed, without strength. You will go to work demoralized; your day will not make sense whatever you do. Abstinence will make everyday life unbearable, and your family will pay the consequences. One thing is certain: you will have to keep reading and practicing until the end. It will be the 30 days in which you will seriously commit yourself to permanently throwing away the cigarette. You can do it, choose.

Usually everything lasts only thirty days from the last cigarette. But your life is going to take an incredible dip during this time. You will not be able to pass body, perhaps you will be forced to take laxatives. You will not enjoy good times like parties or the fun of nightclubs. No smiles. You will think you are a failure no matter what you do. You will think that you do not deserve to be well and that your life is like this and cannot change. You will see smokers everywhere. You will hear the smoke 1 km away, like the sirens call for Ulysses. You will dream of the cigarette that runs after you, that wants to convince you to get back together. You will not be able to pass an exam without a cigarette. You will not be able to deal with a sale without a cigarette. You will have difficulties in relationships, especially in new encounters. You will experience discomfort in almost everything you do daily. You will not even know how to hang a nail without a cigarette in your mouth. All this for only thirty days. Your life will no longer be life. You will lose control of it. You will experience discomfort and disorientation. You will feel fragile, indeed you will be. All this for only 30 days. Overcoming the next thirty days, however, you will be definitively free, I assure you. I give you the guarantee of your success. Accept to commit yourself for 30 days now. If you want to postpone it, next time you will have to reread the entire book. 30 days of sacrifice, suffering, sleepless nights. The smokers you meet will band together against you to start you all over again. You will generate great envy. They will subtly persuade you to smoke. They will pretend that they have forgotten your decision. They will tell you that "It's just a cigarette". There will be those who will tell you that you will recover sooner or later. You will suffer for this. It will make you feel bad. However, by now you know how it works: the smoker does not know how to be alone in discomfort.

What you focus on is amplified

If you think "I don't have to smoke anymore!", then it's extremely possible that you will do it again, because you are focusing on what you want to avoid. Instead, focus your attention on what you want to achieve. Remember when you went to driving school? Or if you have not gone there yet, I anticipate the suggestion that the instructor will give you when you are about to pass between two cars or in any case in a bottleneck. He will tell you to look ahead, where you want to go, and not to look at the obstacles on the road to the right or to the left. It is clear? If you look at the obstacles, you will end up bumping into them. If you look where you want to go, you will pass unscathed. If you think empoweringly, you will exactly arrive where you want to go. If you think about the difficulties, you will be stranded.

Improve your thoughts, every day. Turn them towards wellness. What do you want from your life? What makes you feel good and healthy? These are the only thoughts that you can and must afford, the only ones that must exist in your mind. The more you feed yourself with empowering thoughts, the sooner the old belief will die, the feeling of still being a smoker. You will experience the feeling of being a free, non-smoking person. You know what I mean! Remember the one-way street change? It is about that. Do not remember how it was before!

Accept difficulties

We have already seen that many difficulties arise when one tends to live in the past or in the future. Live in the present and, in to do it, the first step is to accept who you are and what you have. This verb is because it has different meanings according to the context. If we were in a forest, accepting would probably refer to a tree. In your case, on the other hand, it is welcoming who you are. The next step will be to accept, in the sense of tearing apart what you do not like about yourself in order to rebuild it. Eliminate what needs to be replaced and improved. If you are where you are and you have what you have, it is because you have chosen it in one way or another. This can be applied to me too. I have no compassion for myself and I do not intend to have any with you either. Pretending that dissatisfaction and frustration do not exist, you only amplify the difficulties. Like dust under the carpet, discomfort builds up. Accept your condition, whatever it is; is the first step.

Whatever it is. You cannot go back in time. You can never change the past. Never. Get over it. But you can change the way you perceive it. What does it have to do with smoking? It has something to do with it because that's where it originated. Smoking is related to something from your past. Smoking is a way to carry an unsolved part of your past with you. What do you need today? Nothing. I am not telling you that it is useless to downsize the problems; it is not useful to pretend that they do not exist. We need to find a meeting point. Listen to yourselves, stop avoiding problems, respect yourself.

You are the most important person!

Whatever situation you are experiencing, accept it willingly! No one else can do it for you. You cannot think that the situation will work out as you wish, it is just an illusion. Do you know why? You cannot be comfortable with yourself only after things have settled down. It is like going on a diet after reaching your ideal lost shape. First you go on a diet and then you reach a healthy weight. First you get rid of smoking and then you will enjoy excellent health. Improve yourself first and then everything around you will improve. It works like this. And again, how do you know which situation is best for you? If you had really known it, don't you think you would have already reached it? You could tell me that you do not know what it is or answer me instead that you know it and add: "Yes, but...". So, you know it and you are already making up an excuse to justify not taking action to achieve your result. The situation you are in sometimes is the best way to get what you really need. Accept it! I do not know your situation. I would like to meet you personally. However, I can tell you, from my experience and from the people I have followed as a coach, that you cannot achieve a result if you do not change first; you cannot wait for the result and then change. No n is possible.

There is no butterfly that does not pass by the worm and that has not crawled on the ground.

Accept your current situation, it is your best friend. It is telling you that something is wrong, it is suggesting what and how to change. Stay listening and let yourself go. Now is the right time. You must stay there, avoid running away as you usually do.

The emotions

Any emotion you feel has a positive purpose. Emotions exist to guide us to live better, respect ourselves and save-look at us. They have an evolutionary aim. The difficulty arises when an emotion becomes chronic, whatever it is. In this sense, the smoker has learned to inadequately tame emotions. The cigarette is destructive for several reasons, from health to economic spending, but it is useful for the smoker to do "something", to "get a result". It is not easy to manage and be aware of your emotions if no one has taught us. In this chapter we will explore the emotions related to smoking so that you can become more familiar.

Below you will find a classification that does not want to be rigid but only explanatory. Emotions are often composed by intertwining with each other.

Therefore, equip yourself with a pen and paper to answer the questions and do the exercises. Are you ready? Let's see together what the emotions / moods are related to cigarettes: • Anxiety / fear; • Anger / stress / nervousness; • Sadness; • Shame; • Sense of guilt.

Anxiety / Fear

Alex, 28 years old, had tried to quit at least three, five, ten times - so he had expressed himself - over twelve years as a smoker, but he had always put it off. A former sportsman, he was perfectly aware that his breathing had shrunk over time. But he was stronger than him: "This is not the time, I'm too anxious about the university". "It's not a period, I'm too anxious about how things are going with my girlfriend" and so on. Apparently expansive and lover of social life, Alex dragged along with an insecurity that led him to cling to cigarettes in situations in which he felt most vulnerable. He had started smoking as a teenager with friends in a group and was no longer able to quit: "I tell myself that I can't always escape from certain situations or from certain discussions. Smoking comforts me, reassures me, or at least, I think I manage the difficult moment better. But I don't feel free".

Like all emotions, fear is a very useful message. Fear means something! However the smoker, especially the insecure adolescent, soon learns to hide the fear and insecurity (fear of judgment), considered socially unacceptable, by committing to give others the idea of being strong. The cigarette is perfect for him because smoking is a behaviour commonly considered synonymous with safety, a sign of independence and strength in social relationships. Otherwise, from a psychological and personal point of view it denotes *dependence* and *fragility*. With that behaviour, in fact, an incorrect automatic response is created, a kind of "Click and go!". As soon as a situation appears in which fear / discomfort arises unknowingly, the inner spring is triggered towards the cigarette.

Why is this deep and often unconscious response created? Because the smoker managed to overcome a difficult moment, albeit in a clumsy way, always with the cigarette in his hand. At that moment there was a cigarette, and he (or she) did it. So, he ends up linking courage to the cigarette. The cigarette and courage are one and the same in his unconscious mind. It is the confirmation that he cannot overcome his fears alone. So, the cigarette became his solution to fear. Think of the moments in which you take the cigarette, try to understand if the urge to smoke is due to the circumstance, then it is an automatic connection of the "event-sensation-cigarette" type, or if it is due to a nicotine deficiency. Most of the times the causes seem to coincide, it is not easy to understand if it is one or the other. It could also be "boredom": in this case the stimulus takes over to fill the waiting time. If you understand that this is not abstinence, ask yourself:

- What fear is behind it? What is this cigarette useful for?

- What could I do to exorcise fear?

- What would happen if I didn't smoke in this situation?

- Am I able to go it alone without a cigarette?

- What else could I do as an alternative?

_____

_____

_____

Fear is "anticipation of pain". Fear is an internal construction that manages to condition us; it is not so much a real, objective situation, coming from the outside world, as an internal construction, attributable to your culture, the education received or previous experience. To defuse the "Click and go", we must learn to anticipate this sensation, which often creates strong discomfort and incorrect answers. How?

If fear is an anticipation of pain, reflect on everything that worries you at the very thought, or rather, occupies you even before it happens. Thoughts can generate fear, but they are not real, they exist only in your mind. Just change your thoughts to ease the feeling. Anticipate thoughts and, as soon as you are aware of them, work to change them. Faced questions like…

- What if I feel like smoking while I'm driving?

- How will I approach who I like without a cigarette?

- Will I do my job badly, since the cigarette helped me concentrate?
- If I happen to have no cigarettes at night, what will I do?
- How will I fall asleep every night without my cigarette?

...behave smartly: start thinking "what to do if ...". It is not smart to avoid thinking. Predicting your response and training is.

Anger / Stress / Nervousness

Tiziana smoked two packs of cigarettes a day. Since she was young, she had to take upon herself the burden of a difficult family situation, which she had forced her to make some sacrifices. She loved her family very much, but when she thought about everything that had happened, she could not help but light a cigarette and smoke. In addition, there were the heavy pace of work, the boss' requests, the deadlines. When the load of stress became unbearable, the cigarette was her release valve. Until she realized that she was only hurting herself, and that in hindsight she was not the cigarette solving the problems, on the contrary: she often made the situation worse by making her even more nervous. Anger arises from a repressed desire, from an unmet need, from limitations, from invasions from the outside world. Anger serves to establish the boundary between us and the outside world; outlines our intimate area, our freedom of psychological and physical movement. Stress and nervousness have been anticipating and fuelling anger.

If you smoke when you are angry, ask yourself these questions:

- What is the cigarette useful for me in this circumstance?
- What would happen if I didn't smoke it?
- What does this anger want to communicate to me?

The cigarette is used as a sedative. In fact, according to some studies, it only adds to anger, stress and nervousness. When you smoke, the substances contained in the cigarette reach the brain in a few seconds, stimulating the mesolimbic-dopaminergic system. You feel relaxed because dopamine, the so-called *happiness hormone*, is released. But what happens further? The central nervous system is flooded with harmful substances from cigarette combustion, as if a bucket of water were thrown onto electrical circuits; that is, the system suffers damage like a short circuit. In the case of the smoker, the damage equates to increased stress, nervousness and anger, which are the cause of the next cigarette. More precisely, it has been observed that in the life of a smoker there is a kind of point of no return, of transition from a light addiction to a more intense one, in which the cigarette no longer acts as a sedative, but increases the feelings of discomfort and malaise[33]. In order to defuse this mechanism, you can commit to improving your breathing, or even approaching meditation. In any case, make a commitment to stay healthy.

Sadness

Sadness is a request for care. Feeling sad is an issue related to the feeling of abandonment. When you are sad, you feel alone, abandoned. This feeling can often be experienced even if you are amid many people and have many bonds. It is not strictly linked to physical closeness, to frequentation, but to feeling misunderstood, and not feeling loved. This is the case of Adele, do you remember? I talked about her in chapter 7. Adele was a middle-aged woman, tirelessly devoted to her family, who had got into the habit of smoking in moments of sadness: when she felt alone and neglected by her husband and children, she smoked. She withdrew into herself and smoked. Adele made her happiness depend on her family. Not that her family members did not love her, but they were taken from their lives outside the home. Her was an implicit request for attention, for care. But her smoke only increased the distance between her and her husband who, worried about her health, disapproved of her behaviour and demonstrated it with hostile words. When you are sad and you connect the cigarette as an automatic behaviour, the request for help to the outside world is reinforced.

The emotion recalls the cigarette, which in turn reinforces the emotion. Smoking becomes an emergency rocket in the middle of the sea, in the vain hope that someone will notice. As a result, smoking increases the sensation of sadness. So much so that the cigarette has a socializing function, but only among smokers. It is "ghettoizing", so it reinforces the feeling of abandonment and non-understanding on the others' part. The more you smoke, the more you strengthen this mechanism. The solution is to focus just on you, on your self-help, on your 100% commitment and let others lose. Stop blaming others or yourself. Stop now! Repeat with me: stop now!

---

[33] A. Chettoum et al., "Relationship between the degree of dependence to nicotine, and the anxio-depressive levels, according to Fagerstromtest of nicotine dependence and hads test", « Open Journal of Psychiatry», 2012, 2, pp. 235-242. http://file.scirp.org/pdf/OJPsych 20120300007_52526686.pdf

Imagine the road sign in your mind... *stop now!* Focus only on you, you are solely responsible for your wellness and your happiness. When you do not achieve your goals, learn from mistakes, change your attitude, put in even more effort, and try again. Make it a new habit.

Shame

It seems a bit strange that you bring up this emotion, which, to be precise, together with the *sense of guilt* is not an innate and universal emotion (like anger, sadness or joy), but an emotion learned in relation to the environment in which one lives (models, rules and culture). We have learned to mask shame very well. Think of a man's approach to a woman in a club: a cigarette is useful for him to take time, strike up a button and so on. We always go back to the concept of prosthesis that helps. Shame arises from a *devaluation* of oneself with respect to the other. "I am not adequate. I'm wrong". Shame does not hurt others, only yourself. "The others think of me that I am an inadequate person always and, in any case, but in the moments when I smoke this does not happen" a patient told me. The cigarette is not the cause of shame and inadequacy, mind you; the cigarette is only the answer that many have been able to give - or one of the answers - it is an adaptation. Shame is a sign of low self-esteem and low energy: to get rid of the cigarette it will therefore be necessary to work on these aspects.

Sense of guilt

Marzia had grown up in an authoritarian family and she had been a rebellious teenager. Rebel and smoker. She had promised herself that she would leave her parents' house as soon as possible, and so she had. You can imagine the scenes and manipulations on the part of her parents, who never missed an opportunity to accuse her of being an ungrateful daughter, and to try to keep her tied to themselves, even amplifying the seriousness of their health problems. In short, they did everything to ensure that the weight on her daughter was overwhelming. Marzia wanted a life as a free person, as each of us deserves. However, as sometimes happens, she had parents who, with the excuse of love, suffocated her, and did not make her free, and therefore happy. Marzia was now living on her own, but neither her relationship with them had improved, nor she had been able to detach herself from the cigarette. She confided to me that part of her kept blaming herself for having betrayed her parents' expectations, for having been a bad daughter. A part of her always felt lacking in something, and then Marzia lit yet another cigarette. The sense of guilt arises from the lack of respect for one's own moral laws. You think you have harmed or may harm others. These rules exist only in the educational construct. If you connect this emotion to smoking, it is a bit as if with each cigarette you reinforce the belief that you are "wrong" regarding the "rules", that you are inadequate, bad people, able to harm "someone" with your behaviour. This connection is created unconsciously, there is no need for you to repeat it to yourself; it is enough to smoke for your unconscious to be convinced more and more. Why should cigarettes be linked to guilt? The only thing that mitigates the sense of guilt is the expiation of the guilt itself: to pay a penalty, a pledge, to inflict a punishment on oneself. Yes, punishment seems to be the quickest and most frequent response in those suffering from the "serious illness" of guilt. By hurting himself the penitent has the feeling and the conviction of being acquitted. This psychological mechanism concerns those who commit a punishable act because it is offensive towards others or because it violates moral and spiritual precepts. Its scheme is as follows:

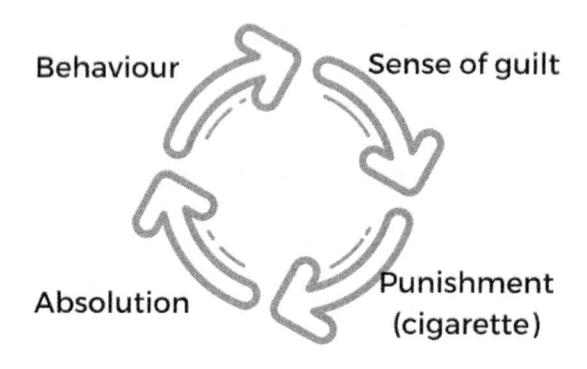

Behaviour → Sense of guilt → Punishment (cigarette) → Absolution

Then, there are those who become paralyzed in acting to avoid harming others, precisely because of the sense of guilt that could derive from it. In their mind they anticipate the scene that will harm others and therefore do not act. This scheme works differently than the previous one which saw an action to be punished. In this scheme, the punishment is the *deprivation* of what one wishes to do or have.

The connection between the cigarette and this pattern appears when the tension is generated between the desire and the negation of the same (as a punishment for having only thought about it) with consequent expiation. The scheme is the following:

Desire → Sense of guilt → Punishment (cigarette) → Absolution → (cycle)

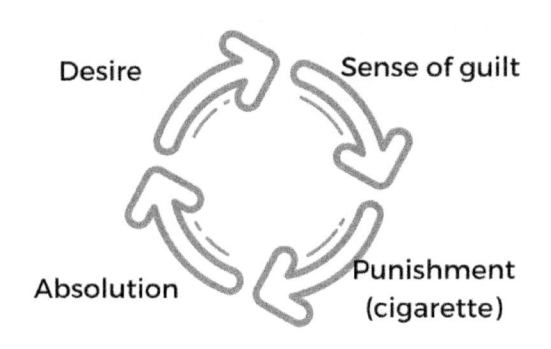

Change perspective and restructure

For each emotion you must change your perspective:

- Hi [*specify which emotion*], what is your function in my life?
- What can I do concretely from now on so that you can be useful?
- What thoughts, feelings and behaviours would you like me to adopt from now on?
- When you manifest in the future, what empowering automatic thoughts and behaviours will it help me to link to my wellness?

Take some time to respond with complete peace of mind. Manage your times, train in the best way. Take notes and write down the answers. Reflect and let yourself go to the process.

Exercise

Restructuring exercise. When you feel one of the emotions just described try to follow this path:

1. Imagine the emotion in question as if it were a thing, give it a shape.

2. Freeze the image. Put it in black and white, make it smaller.

3. Remove the object by destroying the image.

An extra boost towards wellness

Repeat the following exercise whenever you feel you need an extra boost towards your wellness, a moment of relaxation. Learn to predict the situations, limiting and negative thoughts that you might encounter and take precautions with this exercise. It will be your antidote. From now on, whenever you feel overwhelmed by limiting thoughts and situations, simply try to join the index and thumb of the right hand (PIDX), until they disappear.

> Exercise
>
> Think of a pleasant and relaxing moment from your past. A moment of intense joy and wellness. Visualize the scene, listen to the sounds, perceive the smells. Let the sensations of relaxation flood your whole body.
>
> Enter the scene. Maybe you are smiling now. Amplify the sensations you experience, the images you see and the sounds you hear. Experience full pleasure in the whole body.
>
> Imagine every cell in your body enjoying and benefiting from this energy. The energy takes the colour you like best and colours your every cell. Your body is filled with energy and positive sensations. Press right hand index and thumb (PIDX). Repeat for 5 times. Now, recall a stressful situation that makes you feel bad. Think about it and concentrate on the sensations associated with it, retrace the images and listen to the sounds, your internal dialogue. Press the index finger and thumb of the left hand (PISX). Repeat 5 times.
>
> With each repetition, feel and perceive between the fingers of the left hand a pebble that grows more and more. Looking closer, you realize that it is an ice cube. Look up and see before you a regenerating fire. Take the cube you have between the fingers of your left hand and bring it to the fire. That cube contains all your anxieties, discomfort, negative feelings of heaviness and stress that you have accumulated; it's all there, concentrated in that cube. Approaching it to the fire, it begins to melt.
>
> Feel that the cube is gradually reduced until it disappears completely. *Shh*, it melted! Repeat for 5 times. Now, you feel a sensation of lightness, you have freed yourself from the weights and join the index and thumb of the right hand (PIDX) while all the constructive, positive sensations are amplified; energy grows: every

> cell in your body is coloured with your favourite colour and you feel and see your best. Repeat for 5 times.

Only one

If you are thinking that every now and then you can only smoke one cigarette, you are wrong! You would still be a smoker. A thief is always a thief, whether he steals 1 million euros or takes only 10 euros. Evil, large or small, whether it is a packet or "a single cigarette", is always evil. Saying "one cigarette" is a trap that is about to snap. It is the pattern that reappears. Now you have no more excuses, you know very well how it will end. You will resume smoking for sure. When you think like this, tell yourself:

> "Thanks for reminding me of my commitment!
>
> I am a non-smoker; I have never smoked! ".
>
> "I'm finally free!".

If someone invites you to smoke, you can answer:

> "No thanks! I am a non-smoker! "

The true non-smoker who used to smoke never starts again. Those who start over have never stopped within themselves. He never changed thought patterns, feelings and behaviours. The new non-smoker feels like he has never smoked, he is reborn. There is no such thing as "smoking just one", because it is as if it were the first. Smoking your first cigarette with this new awareness is silly, it does not make any sense. Do you agree with me? In adolescence it made sense. Not anymore now. The thought of starting to smoke is unpleasant.

The thought of wellness is strong, you know it, you know what I am talking about.

If you feel the urge to smoke, ask yourself these questions - it will pass instantly, because the conditioned mind will become aware:

- If you helped a person following a car accident, would you give them a cigarette as a sedative while waiting for the ambulance?

- If your wife, who has never smoked, lost her job, would you offer her a cigarette to make her feel better?

- If a child fell in front of you and peeled his knee, would you give him a cigarette to comfort him?

- If your daughter were to take an exam, would you give her a cigarette to smoke before entering the classroom to perform better?

- If your non-smoker collaborator achieved the best team result, would you reward him with a cigarette?

No, no, and again no! You would never use a cigarette to make a person feel better, because it does not make anyone feel better. It only makes nicotine addicts, cigarette addicts, feel less worse. A hug, affection, love, friendship, trust in others: this is what makes people feel good.

First you and then me

Typically the smoker waits for some other person to have achieved the same result before him to act. If you have this thought, forget it, keep smoking. This thought indicates a weak, fragile, irresponsible person who will never take his life in hand. Anyone who always finds excuses in front of solutions is a loser. The "You First, Then Me" story is just a childish excuse. You do not need it. I have learned to know you and I see that you are willing to free yourself from the cigarette. William, a 50-year-old gentleman, came to me to find out more about how I could help him quit smoking. After 20 minutes of meeting, he told me that a friend of his had already been to me.

Logically, I thought that his friend had stopped smoking, that he was there thanks to the evident testimony of his friend. I was sure about that. It was not like that; his friend was still smoking. This struck me a lot. I was faced with a responsible person. He was aware that he and his friend were two different people, with equally different motives. He chose to be followed regardless of his friend's failure. He really wanted to be okay. Those who wait for others to move forward are preparing for failure and to settle for crumbs.

Americans say, "go first" which means "go first", addressing themselves. Be an example. Starting, not putting off, getting a result, learning and guiding others. I have lost count of those who have told me: "If I stop, hundreds of people will come!". I swear to you, nobody ever came, even though they stopped. And many companions said, "If my friend stops, I'll come soon after too!". Never happened. Never. Although the friend had stopped. The smoker is a serial liar. He stays under cover in the second row just to continue smoking.

Post termination

30 days after the last cigarette, physical addiction is no longer a problem. You cannot have any physical dependence. The perception of being smoke-free comes around the ninetieth day. To be honest, this feeling could also come later, however, from the physiological point of view, after 30 days you are already out of addiction. Jack Mangiaracina, in his book *Curare il fumo 34*, explains how smoking involves a neuronal change in the brain, increasing the number of nicotinic receptors. Within one year of the cessation there is the possibility to resume with the same number of cigarettes smoked before it, because the receptors remain active for that period. This does not mean that the stimulus remains. The need for nicotine disappears almost immediately after cessation. Only the predisposition remains; the risk of relapse is higher only if, for the reasons mentioned above, one indulges in it and starts smoking again. This shouldn't discourage you: it certainly doesn't have to pass a year! Feel free now! However, at an indicative level, I can tell you that many people I followed in a coaching path confirmed to me that they had reached the full conviction that they were free from smoking about three months after the last cigarette.

Set the beginning if you have not done it yet. Is it scary? For someone, yes, it is. We are almost at the end of the book, but the best is yet to come! "Now what should I do... throw the package?", "... Stop?" Are you thinking this? If it has not happened yet, do it now. All anti-smoking experts give the same advice: set the date! However, I would add that, in my experience, the date itself is of little use if the inner spring is not triggered. I do not want to swear that on a specific date you will stop, you will feel within yourself if it is about to happen and then you will intensify the exercises and the reading of the book until the impulse is triggered. As soon as it happens, it will be forever.

Your recurring phrase will be: "The day is coming! The date is in my mind and is about to reveal itself". Reread the book and go through it again with more effort. It's a question of training. Amplify everything you do, multiply the exercises. Be consistent, determined and disciplined. Take a deep breath: "The day is coming! The date is in my mind and is about to reveal itself". Always repeat it, every time you do it, the date becomes clearer and clearer, until you identify a specific day and that will be. It may not be a distant day, but a near moment. The more you tell yourself that the day is coming, the more likely it is to happen, and you will be willing to welcome it. It's a good way to prepare for change. Focus!

---

[34] G. Mangiaracina, Curare il fumo. Manuale per smettere di fumare, edup Edizioni, 2007 Rome.

Observe and interview

Work on this pattern, either writing it here or reproducing it on a larger sheet. Observe all smokers you meet; pay close attention to the way they speak and move as well as the sensations they transmit to you. Compare what you have read so far with their behaviours. You will notice all the attitudes of insecurity, fear, anger, etc. in some circumstances. You will see the smoker under another guise. Insert everything positive you find in the smoker's observation under the sign (+) and everything you find negative under the sign (-).

+	−

You will receive lots of useful information to improve yourself further. Dwell on different situations and people to have more models to learn from. Know that you are unconsciously projecting what you think about yourself as a smoker onto them. This exercise is very useful because it makes you more and more aware: it amplifies the positive aspects of quitting and the negative aspects of continuing to smoke. After doing this exercise, interview those who no longer smoke today. Ask them what positives and negatives they found without the cigarette.

+	−

Become a master

If you really want to make a difference, become strong and smoke-free, I suggest a further step: become a master, lead others. A kind of mentors who lead other smokers to break free. When you teach others, you inevitably become what you say and do. Teaching who you are helps you become even more competent. You have your own example; you know what to do and how to be non-smokers. We need to be consistent and be an example. Some would like to pass for masters only with the theory, you have the practice.

The teacher appears when the student is ready. Meet your students and help them become masters themselves. You can all count with your thoughts, your new identity, with the desire for wellness and with the enthusiasm to free others from the trap of cigarettes. The teacher does not force, he does not criticize. Share your knowledge with all smokers, help them be more aware. Talk to them about how you feel without a cigarette and how you managed to do it, about your efforts. Let them understand that this way you live better and that they too can. Tell us how difficult it was on the one hand and fun on the other. Tell them what you have learned. Transmit your life experience, what happened inside you, how you face situations today. Talk about your new awareness, the courage you did not think you had. You had some images in your previous life when you smoked and the vision you have as a free person. Now, that you are finally a free person, help others. By doing this you will feel more and more free: this is the extraordinary sensation. *You* are the most important people; you have improved yourself and continue to do so consistently every day. Each step forward empowers you to help those who are one step behind. Help those who cannot free themselves from smoking, be their mentors. The better you become as a teacher, the more people who will accept your suggestions will be your support.

They will choose you. Now, think of a person you would like to help quit smoking. Get started. It is a commitment to you and to her. Help her. Then, there will be two of you and so on. Infect others with your desire for wellness! Perhaps not everyone will choose like you to be free, non-smokers, but those who do will be grateful to you. My biggest motivation has always been the belief that by making even one person quit smoking, I would certainly save their life. Think about this too: you can save some life.

Thank you! This is for you. For all the patience, desire and commitment you have put in so far.

Thanks for all who you will help!

DOWNLOAD YOUR FREE BONUS

Click on this link or type this https://bityl.co/NJIP and visit the website reserved only for those who have purchased Quit smoking easily, just like you! Enter your email and you will immediately receive the link.

Download and print the exercise cards for the best result

If you liked this book we ask you to put in your best review. Thank you for your helpfulness!

US> https://bit.ly/3H0SQGC

CA> https://bit.ly/4aERy1y

UK> https://bit.ly/48zgg1D

AU> https://bit.ly/48CLQf3

CONCLUSION

Well, good. If we have come this far it means that you have done a great job.

Throughout these pages we have carried out a process of knowledge and awareness that has helped you to change your perspective regarding the problem of smoking, on yourself and on others. Beliefs and identity were the aspects most called into question; but indirectly, the speech also touched on values such as family, affections, love, wellness, self-esteem.

Smoking was, has always been and always will be something different from you and your identity. Thanks to targeted questions, you were able to look at the latter from a new perspective, to place yourself as an aware spectator of what you did and were doing every day in relation to cigarettes. You have travelled in time and you have rewritten - or at least revised and modified - the perceptions and sensations related to the moments in which those limiting beliefs that are the cause of the cigarette's imprisonment were formed. At this point, some of you will probably feel a bit lost. Better this way, because "change encounters less resistance in bewilderment", as Mary told me, in hindsight: mother, wife, "cleaning lady and longshoreman", as she preferred to present herself at our first meeting, when this he could not know. It is certainly one of the most incredible and meaningful stories I came across. 42 years old, intelligent, charming and engaging woman; however, she looked dull, tired and she thought everything was but interesting. Mary also had a great desire to change a life in which she did not even know how it ended. Does any of you sound familiar?

Mary had three strong convictions:

1. Her only freedom was the cigarette, and she had nothing else left. It could not have been otherwise now. She realized that the only thing she believed she could exercise control over was smoking, and she was under the illusion that she was managing her own connection with the cigarette.

2. She felt incapable and helpless in the face of life, resigned.

And very, very unhappy. Although she possessed all the social indicators of happiness (degree, home, job, money, family), she did not feel valued as a person, covering all her roles solely and exclusively for the well-being of others.

3. Her biggest fear was that any change would certainly worsen her already troubled existence. She was so afraid that the very thought of her made her feel unwell.

Her identity was projected to make her increasingly more unhappy every day. Thus, as a result, her behaviours are increasingly pedantic, stressful, disheartening. Rivers of cigarettes followed. But, at this point in the book, it is very clear to you that the cigarette question is not the real problem, but a consequence, the result of a bad life. Mary decided to follow the suggestions in this book. She read all the exercises, but then focused only on a few that she considered fundamental for her. With effort, effort and commitment. Because behind great resistance there is the most important, profound and significant change for everyone's wellness. As a result of our work together, Mary made some important life choices. I let her tell you directly how she made her, how she feels and what her gain has been thanks to have undertaken perhaps the greatest transformation of her life. This change in her took months to snap and take shape:

«I have always been subject to others. Apparently, I was free, but everything I did I think I did to make others happy and not myself. The cigarette was my escape valve, the only thing I thought I could control. But once again I realized that I wasn't free, but that I was addicted to the cigarette. We often think that in order to feel good it is others who must change, but in my case, I had to change as a person. For my well-being, I had to become another person, a woman who loves herself and who respects herself. Without the path taken with Han I would not have been able to understand it. At first, I was uncertain because I thought it was something for selfish people: but then I realized that if I wasn't well at first, even those around me would not be well. How did it happen? One day Han asked me: "Do you really want a happy life and pass on your well-being to others or do you prefer to remain in this condition and contribute to the malaise of those you love?". This was my spring. From this question I changed my whole life, some things gradually, others sharply and suddenly. I started to dig inside myself and rediscover my dreams, and my needs, to understand who I really was and who I wanted to become. I have upset delicate, fundamental parts of my life as a wife and mother. I did it for myself, and after a first pain, it turned out to be the best gift I could give to me and my family. Today I know what I want, and I live better. Growing up, changing is necessary to feel good. The routine, the stillness only led you to feel bad and to smoke more and more cigarettes. The? I have never smoked! Thank you».

The work we did was really demanding and certainly, despite having been good, I suggest you re-read the book, maybe only those paragraphs that you think have been particularly helpful, and repeat the exercises, especially in the first months but also later in time: every now and then take it in your hand and give it a dusting. I myself reread the useful books several times, those that have improved me, for two reasons: the first is that there is really a need to repeat in order to assimilate; the second is that over time I myself have changed and understand, interpret and assimilate the same information in a different and effective way. You also understood that you can do it yourself, that the rest are just excuses that keep you from freeing yourself from the cigarette. All, none excluded. Finally, we have applied techniques and strategies to rehabilitate well-being, to a healthy lifestyle and to break the unhealthy habit of smoking, knowing however that with this book or by any other means you cannot really stop if first you do not make this decision and if you do not make the effort to change every day. You must work on all these aspects.

Well, I think I have told you everything you need to know and have provided you with enough ideas and solicitations. Over time, some may find it helpful to receive support, and you may offer it yourself, in reciprocity. You may be going through more difficult times than expected or be tempted by possible relapses.

Remember that conditioning for well-being is like training your muscles: you need perspective, continuity and training. You must work your mental muscles by putting into practice what you now know, developing strength, energy and new empowering abilities. Only you have the power to make a difference in your life.

I would like to get to know you all personally and, who knows, one day it might even happen. A sincere hug and full of energy, because I know you will need it.

Thanks again for believing in me.

I reciprocate, I believe in you!

AUTHOR

Han Carrel (1978) is a *coach*. He has been working in the field of personal growth for over sixteen years. With an always attentive look at the most innovative methods of improvement, effective communication and coaching for psychophysical well-being.

WOULD YOU LIKE TO RECEIVE NEW BOOKS FOR FREE? Sign up now for our newsletter to receive new books and bonuses for free! (*Limited number of subscriptions*)

We are waiting for you

Printed in Great Britain
by Amazon